MIKE

MAKE

INSIDE HOME RENOVATION WITH
CANADA'S MOST TRUSTED CONTRACTOR

HOLMES IT RIGHT®

THE HOLMES GROUP
President Mike Holmes
CEO Michael Quast
Director of Communications Liza Drozdov
Creative/Content Manager Mark Bernardi
Director, Holmes Homes Seth Atkins

TIME HOME ENTERTAINMENT
Publisher Richard Fraiman
Vice President, Business Development & Strategy Steven Sandonato
Executive Director, Marketing Services Carol Pittard
Executive Director, Retail & Special Sales Tom Mifsud
Executive Director, New Product Development Peter Harper
Director, Bookazine Development & Marketing Laura Adam
Publishing Director Joy Butts
Finance Director Glenn Buonocore
Assistant General Counsel Helen Wan
Design & Prepress Manager Anne-Michelle Gallero
Book Production Manager Susan Chodakiewicz

Published by Time Home Entertainment Inc.

Originally published in hardcover by Collins: 2006
This trade paperback edition: 2011

Make It Right® is a registered trademark of Make It Right Licensing Ltd.

Published by Time Home Entertainment Inc.
135 West 50th Street
New York, New York 10020

ISBN 13: 978-1-60320-194-0   ISBN 10: 1-60320-194-7

DWF 9 8 7 6 5 4 3 2

Printed and bound in the United States

For my dad.

CONTENTS

MIKE HOLMES
MAKE IT RIGHT

"Mike, if you're going to do something, do it right the first time"

It was something my father always said to me. And it was something he believed in—something that he lived. He was a true jack-of-all-trades. He had trained as a plumber, then worked at General Motors for his whole adult life, eventually becoming a second-class engineer. But from the time I was about 3 years old, all my memories of him working take place at our family's house in Toronto's East End. I was always beside him, watching, infatuated with his ability to change things—to take down walls or redo our house's plumbing. He realized I wasn't going away, so he started to teach me. "Dad, let me do it, let me try it," I used to say. Eventually he let me, overseeing everything I did. By the time I was six, I had rewired the whole house under his supervision. I chose where to run the wires, put them through the receptacle boxes and switches, and wired the whole thing together. For me, it was a totally exciting thing to do. When I wasn't working on the house, I was taking apart my toys. "Why are you taking them apart?" my dad would ask. "I want to know how they're put together," I'd tell him. Later I was building go-karts, and I put together a trailer that was so big it had to be pulled by two bicycles. When I was 8 or 9, I built a three-bedroom tree house and freaked my dad out because I'd used every single nail and piece of lumber that he had hanging around the house. > > >

My dad and I worked on our house constantly, and I picked up how to do things the proper way. One time I was helping him gut a room. Being young and foolish, I was just ripping things down, letting the floor get covered with debris. He said I should stop and clean it up, but I said I was almost done and I would clean it up later. Then I grabbed a chair instead of a ladder—and put it on a pile of debris. I didn't realize that the debris was covering up a hole where we had taken out a hot air register. When I stood up on the chair to pull the rest of the ceiling down, one chair leg went into the hole. I lost my balance, landed on the chair, broke it, and cut myself big time.

The first thing my dad said to me was, "Are you okay?" The second was, "Does that teach you anything?"

In addition to working on our house, my dad was always being asked to work on other people's homes, to come in and help them—something he found very hard to refuse. After a few years he started telling them, "Hire my son." When I was 12 years old, I did my first basement renovation. It was my uncle's house, and my dad knew I could do it. I did the whole thing—the panelling, the stairs, the dropped ceiling, everything.

I kept working and learning. By the time I was 19, I was being offered a lot of money to run a renovation company with 14 employees. We built two custom homes and completed major renovations, including many kitchens and bathrooms. I talked to a lot of pros, and I learned from them. With every home I went into, I learned more. And the more I learned, the more I wanted to let homeowners know what was going on, too. I'd always grab the homeowner and say, "Hey, see what I found here? This is the problem, this is why it's happening, and this is how it should have been done." I guess that was the beginning of my career as a real pro contractor, a contractor who wanted to let homeowners know, each and every time I priced a job, why we do what we do and why it's important to use the right products. I didn't really think it would have anything to do with my future as a contractor, especially on TV, but I began to see that my impulse was to teach others what I knew.

Two and half years later, I realized it was time to go into business on my own. One job followed another, including an 18,000-square-foot showroom for La-Z-Boy—probably the biggest project I had ever done. Every once in a while I'd bring my dad in to take a look at the projects I was doing, just because I respected and loved him so much. When I was about 24, I designed and completed a $52,000 bathroom, and I brought my father in to see the job. I'll never forget what he said. He actually swore and was upset. I was a little stunned by his reaction and asked him what was the matter. He said, "I can't believe what you've done. You've created a bathroom far beyond anything I could ever see or do." I said, "What are you talking about? You can do this, Dad—you can do it in your sleep." He replied, "Mike, you've taken everything I've taught you and taken it to the next level. You know codes I've never even heard of." That was the day I knew my father was proud of me, and it's a day I'll never forget.

The most important lesson I learned from my father wasn't about wiring or plumbing or carpentry. It was about doing things right. He cared about what he did, and so for him, doing something right wasn't just a business practice, it was about who you were as a person, and how you treated others. My dad is gone now, but that lesson has stayed with me. I've tried to carry it into everything I have done, from renovating houses to writing this book. I have always tried to get it right the first time.

Dad, this is for you.

CHAPTER ONE
Slow Down

The more you know, the better your home will be

So you're planning a renovation. Maybe you've been thumbing through decorating magazines, looking at the latest kitchens, with their fantastic stone countertops and the most amazing new stainless-steel appliances. Or you've seen a nice bathroom on a TV show, with a big tub and flashy fittings. Or someone on your street has turned their old basement into a fantastic home entertainment center.

Or it might be your dreams are a little more down to earth. You've found a house in the right neighborhood, but it needs work—the bathroom is tiny, and the kitchen is looking a little tired. Or the kids are getting a bit older and you want to turn your basement into a place for them to play. Whether you are going wild or taking a simpler approach, a renovation is a good chance to really put your stamp on your home. >>>

Our problem today is that when we want something, we want it right away

Renovations can seem expensive, but they pay off in the long run. Check with your local real estate agent; chances are you'll find that a mid-range kitchen remodel will earn back about 72% of the money you spent on it. And a mid-range bathroom remodel will get you back about 71%. It's the same with other renovations: an addition, if it is a family room, will make you back about 62% of its cost, and a finished basement will earn back about 70%. These are good financial arguments for fixing up your home.

Lately I've been hearing a lot of comments from homeowners who are deathly afraid of doing any type of renovation, and even more afraid of buying a brand-new home. I don't want you to be afraid. I want you to be informed when you make decisions about the single most expensive investment in your life: your home. I want you to have the tools and the knowledge that you need to deal with contractors and builders. The more you know, the better your home will be. And that's just as simple as ABC. If it's built right, it lasts longer.

Step One: Slow Down

One problem today is that when we want something, we want it right away. When we want a burger, we just go to McDonald's. And when we want a new kitchen, we think we can just pick it up.

Renovating isn't like that. If you are planning a renovation, slow down. The work can't start tomorrow, and you can't hire the first person who comes through your door. We're looking at a process that can take up to a year before the renovation itself begins. You must take the time to educate yourself before you even pick up the phone to call a contractor.

First, be sure that you've spent enough time living in your home to determine what you like and what you want to change. You usually need at least a year in a house—four seasons, day and night—to figure that out. Just like people, homes have personalities, and you should take the time to get to know your home's personality before diving in to make major design changes. In other words, sleep on it.

Whether you've just moved in or you've lived there practically forever, spend some time really educating yourself about what possibilities there are for redesigning your home or any part of it. Read design books and magazines. Go to the big box stores and take their seminars to learn about techniques. Surf the Web to find out about new products and why you might want to use them. Learn how much they cost.

And, of course, read this book.

Bathrooms: Often small but always complex

Renovations are complex. A bathroom reno requires skilled plumbing, electrical, and structural work. Tiles, fixtures, and faucets will work only as well as what's behind them.

In my more than 25 years in this business, I have done hundreds and hundreds of renovations. I'm going to walk you through the process. If you slow down and educate yourself, you'll have a better idea of what it is you want and what you need, so that when you're ready to call in contractors, you can determine if they know what they're talking about and if they're right for you and your job.

Step Two: Plan, Plan, and Plan Some More

It's probably fair to say that most renovations come about for a combination of practical and aesthetic reasons. You're tired of cooking in that poorly designed, dingy kitchen with no storage space, let's say—and besides, you sure would like to have a fabulous-looking kitchen like the one you saw in that design magazine last week.

Whatever your reasons, plan your renovation down to the last detail, being realistic about what you'll really need and how much it will cost. Here's a brief list of what you should try to accomplish during the planning stage:

► ► ► **Make a wish list of exactly what you want.** You probably have lots of ideas; now, consult books, magazines, and maybe an interior designer or architect to help flesh out your ideas. Think in terms of layout, space, storage, fixtures, and finishes. Educate yourself about the best products available today—the ones that will ensure that your home is waterproof, energy-efficient, long-lasting, and attractive.

► ► ► **Take a thorough inventory of your home,** either by hiring a home inspector or by using chapters 3 and 4 of this book. You might also consult a plumber, electrician, or heating/cooling/air-conditioning (HVAC) expert to help you assess the state of your home's mechanical systems. Any or all of these steps will help you determine what underlying issues you may be facing. Be prepared to spend on these fundamentals before you splurge on expensive finishes.

► ► ► **Determine how much money you can afford to spend,** whether you get there by saving or by borrowing.

A renovation is a good time to improve the insulation in your house. If you're gutting your exterior walls, think about getting spray foam insulation. It's the best kind out there.

Lots of banks and trust companies will loan you money for home improvements. Be careful to consider, though, how the repayment costs will affect your monthly budget. With a total cost figure in mind, take another look at your wish list and, if necessary, make it more realistic.

▶ ▶ ▶ **Begin compiling a list of the various professionals you might want to work with** for your renovation. The most important one, of course, is your general contractor. The next chapter will tell you what to look for in a general contractor and will also discuss the role of design professionals such as architects, engineers, and interior designers.

▶ ▶ ▶ **Decide when your renovation will best fit into your personal and family life,** and coordinate your schedule with your contractor's.

As you go through the planning stages, you'll want answers to some key questions: What can you expect to pay, and how long will it take to finish the work? Here is a list of some of the most popular renovations and the time they generally take once the work begins. Bear in mind, always, that these are rough estimates. A number of factors—the age of your house, for example—can affect these times. And keep in mind that prices are always rising.

KITCHENS

A kitchen would cost, on average, $10,000 to $40,000, and the installation should take about two weeks once you have all the supplies in place: countertop, cabinets, flooring. Even if you're looking at an incredibly fancy kitchen, I would still say it shouldn't take more than two weeks of actual contractor's time on the job site.

BATHROOMS

Bathrooms generally cost between $10,000 and $20,000 to do. I've personally done bathrooms for $50,000, but those are the extreme. As far as time goes, your average bathroom should take you no more than two weeks when all the materials are ready. Real pros, honestly, could probably do it in seven working days. Any more than two weeks—or less than seven days—and you should get suspicious. Either the contractor doesn't know what he's doing, or he isn't doing the job properly.

BASEMENTS

A basement is a lot more money: $30,000 on average. Some of people think they can get it done for $15,000 or even less. Well, you can't. If you know of people who did this, they likely didn't get a permit and the contractor didn't make a lot of the upgrades that would have been necessary if they had a permit. Even the average of $30,000 is a little misleading. If, for example, you want to lower the floor in your basement, that can add incredibly to the cost—double it, in fact.

ADDITIONS

How much should it cost to put an addition on your home? Anywhere from $90 a square foot right up to $360 a square foot. The average is $120 a square foot. This is not a Taj Mahal. This will give you the minimum code requirements—carpet, vinyl flooring, possibly some ceramic in your bathroom, etc. That means that if you are planning an 800-square-foot addition—and that is about average—you're looking at around $100,000. And this should take anywhere from three to four months. Any of the ridiculous amounts of time that you sometimes hear

It could take as long—and often much longer—to find the right contractor as it takes to do the actual job

for a renovation—a year, a year and a half—are just that: ridiculous.

For simpler home improvements, such as decks and fences, there are a couple of loose estimates that will help you judge a contractor's quote. The rule for a deck is generally $15 a square foot without railings or stairs; the general rule for fences is $12 per foot of fence. Note that these are absolute bare minimums. Based on these, an 8' x 10' deck would cost $1200. These are figures that contractors use to get in your house—then they add extras. Do you want pretty? It'll cost you. But all that said, it is useful to have at least a ballpark figure to work with.

These are all helpful starting points. In later chapters we'll talk a bit more about costs and times, and in the next chapter, on hiring your contractor, I'll give you a good rule of thumb for calculating costs even more carefully.

If you bring in outside help, like a designer, engineer, or architect, you need to factor in their fees. How much is a designer? On average, $5,000 a job. An engineer is on average $5,000 to $10,000 a job, and an architect is anywhere from $5,000 to $20,000, even up to $60,000,

depending on the size of your project.

Do you really need to spend the money that way? No matter what the answer—no matter who does the planning or helps you with it—the job must be planned out carefully, down to the last detail.

Step Three: Hire the Right People

When I ask most people what they expect when they're about to start a renovation, the first words out of their mouths are usually something like this: "It's going to cost more than expected, and it's going to take forever." Then, they add, they'll probably run into problems with the contractor, and they don't know if they can handle the stress. What I hear is all negative.

► ► ► Let me assure you right now: You can do this—you can handle it. I'm not going to minimize how tough it can be to get a renovation done right, of course; it's definitely a challenge. Personally, I love challenges. But whether you love challenges or not is beside the point if you've decided you want that renovation done. You want the end result?

Then you've got to take up the challenge and go through the process to make it happen—to make it right.

But let me repeat: You can do it. For every step of a renovation, there is a process to follow, and I'm going to show you what that process is, every step of the way. As we move along, I'm going to take you into the process in greater and greater detail, but for now let's just look at the basics. Step one, as I've said, is slowing down and educating yourself. If you're reading this book, you're already moving ahead with that.

After planning, the next step has to do with hiring the right people for the job. A common mistake many homeowners make is trusting other people completely—before they've earned that trust—and not trusting themselves. They want to hire the first guy who walks in their door, especially if he's eager to get started. But if you've educated yourself first, by the time you start speaking to general contractors you'll know exactly what you want and you'll have a pretty good idea of what has to be done to get it. Don't let yourself be talked into something because you didn't have the confidence to trust your own judgment or your own instincts.

▶ ▶ ▶ **The most important thing to know about finding the right contractor is this:** It could take as long—and often much longer—to find the right contractor as to do the actual job. Finding the right contractor to work on your renovation, no matter how big or small it may be, is something that takes a lot of legwork—phone calls, checking references, visiting other jobs done by the contractors you're considering. I'll go into detail about this in chapter 2, but for now, just get used to the idea that finding a contractor is a big and time-consuming part of any job. Don't rush it, and don't try

to get around it. Of course you want to spend your money wisely, so start by hiring the right people for the right job for the right price. That's spending your money right.

Step Four: Go Legal and Go Safe: Get the Permits You Need, and Always Exceed Building Code

Almost any renovation you might have in mind will require a permit of some kind. I know, it sounds like a drag, doesn't it? But in fact, permits—and the people at City Hall who give them out (for a cost)—are good for you. Much like insurance, they protect you and your investment. Here's how to do it.

When you get a permit, members of the inspections departments in your municipality look carefully at the drawings and specifications you've brought in. In some cases, a simple hand-drawn sketch will do, but depending on your state and municipality or the complexity of the job, you may need to get the drawings drawn by an engineer or a registered architect. Check with your local building and planning department. Before granting your permit, the city's specialists will make sure that your renovation is going to meet the requirements laid down in the building code.

The building code, which deals with the strength of the house's frame and foundation and lots of other things, sets out the lowest standards that will ensure that a house is going to be safe and secure. While there are similarities in all U.S. building codes, they can vary from state to state and even within towns or cities in each state. There will be special provisions in some regions to protect against local dangers, such as earthquakes or hurricanes. There are separate

TIP

Always go better than code

As useful as the building code is in terms of ensuring safety, it's not enough. Why? Because the building code doesn't set standards that will necessarily give you long-term comfort or lasting value. That's not its job. Its primary job is to ensure that houses are safe and to help keep house prices reasonable by setting out the minimum that has to be done. But we can and we must build better.

For example, minimum code in most places specifies that 2" x 8" floor joists can be set on 16" centers, with a maximum span (length) of 12 feet. Sure, this is safe, even if you have a lot of people standing on the floor. But bounce up and down in the middle of this floor, and every lamp in the room will shake. Builders in general decided, in the end, to do better than that; they started setting those joists only 12 inches apart. Why? Complaints from new-home buyers were coming in fast and furious (and those complaints were costly to deal with). Their tile floors were cracking because the support for the floor underneath wasn't strong enough, even though the floor was built to code.

If I were to offer you a choice between minimum code and spending a few thousand dollars more so that your tiles didn't crack or the area around your windows was properly insulated or your basement was totally watertight, would you spend the extra money? Of course you would. In the long run, you would have a stronger, more efficient, and more valuable home. Always go for more than code. You will never regret it.

Cracked tile and grout in a kitchen with floor joists built to code.

codes that deal with minimum standards for a home's plumbing and electrical system, as well. When an inspector comes to look at a new house or a finished renovation project, the project is approved on the basis of meeting code.

A building permit is formal permission to proceed with your renovation. A permit outlines what the owners are doing, from changes to the structure to where the plumbing will go and how it's going to be run. Having a permit does not mean the work is going to be beautiful, it does not mean it is going to be level, and it does not mean it is going to be square. What the permit shows is that your planned renovation or upgrade complies with the building code and local planning ordinances.

Once the permit is approved and you've posted it in a window on the job site, you'll need to make sure that inspections are done. Building permits tell us what we can build; it is the building inspector's job to make sure the contractor did what the permit allowed and did it properly. A lot of homeowners worry about visits by the building inspector, but inspectors can be your allies.

▶ ▶ ▶ **Depending on where you live, you may have four different building inspectors** coming to your home, one each to cover the electrical, the plumbing, the structural work, and the HVAC. Or there may be only one inspector to take care of everything, which is the case in a lot of smaller towns.

The inspector (or inspectors) will likely visit your house more than once, to do their inspection in stages. As an example, if you were building an addition, a building inspector would first want to see footings, would come back later to look at the foundation, and would generally

check on all aspects of the structure as the addition progressed, finally checking on the insulation. In some jurisdictions, there will also be a drywall inspection and a final inspection.

How many times exactly the inspector goes through depends on the complexity of the job. Don't worry: Your permit will outline exactly when you need inspections, as well as who you must call to set them up. And once you've made that first contact with the inspectors, they will tell you when another inspection is required. If they don't, ask.

▶ ▶ ▶ **Both you and your contractor should be there whenever an inspector comes to call**—if there are four different building inspectors, make sure that you are there for the four different appointments. You both need to know if there are any problems to be rectified, and your contractor needs to know that you know. This keeps him from telling you that everything was fine even when it wasn't. Do not trust the word of anyone but the inspector. How many times have I heard a homeowner with a disaster on his hands say, "Oh, they said everything had passed," only to find out the inspector had never been there at all. Do not—repeat, do not—go any further at each stage, or allow your contractor to go any further, without confirming it with your building inspector.

▶ ▶ ▶ **An inspection's primary purpose is to ensure that minimum code is being met by your contractor,** but it's useful for other reasons, too. As the homeowner, you are assured that the job specifications pass muster, making you confident when it comes time to resell your home. This is a definite selling point for prospective buyers because it gives them peace of mind about the quality of your renovations. (You'll want to hang on to all permits and

Mike's TIP

Do I have to get a permit?

Most of the time, the answer is yes. At the very least, you should start by asking your municipal government the question. You will usually find there is a building and planning department to oversee such things.

Here are some examples of jobs that almost always require a permit:

- Building a deck
- Adding a new residential dwelling unit, such as a suite in the basement or attic
- Doing structural work, such as repairing, altering, or adding to your house's floor framing, roof framing, or any of their supporting elements
- Gutting a building
- Adding or enlarging a window
- Installing a hot tub or swimming pool
- Creating or altering an entrance/exit

The point here is that most jobs on your house, with the exception of surface changes, such as painting walls or putting up shelves, are going to require a permit. Don't tempt fate—or your local building inspector, who'll be looking for job sites without permits posted in the window, and who won't hesitate to slap you with a fine and a stop-work order.

Slow down, get the permit, make it right.

inspection reports; these create a "map" of your house that will be invaluable to you.) As well, inspections allow the government keep a record of what improvements you have made, which means your home can be reassessed and could be taxed higher in the future. Some people skip inspections to try to avoid higher taxes, but it's not worth the risk of a bad, or even unsafe, renovation.

Let's talk more about when you need permits and how you go about getting them. If your contractor is going to do a simple facelift—a new sink and toilet for your bathroom, for example—then you almost certainly do not need a building permit. But if you plan on changing the electrical, if you are going to get in there and start playing with plumbing or ventilation, or if you want to do work on your home's structure, you will need permits. If you plan to demolish your home or gut the inside of it, that requires a permit, too.

If you're not sure whether what you plan requires a permit, get in touch with your local government—they will tell you. They'll also tell you what it will cost. The cost of a permit is dependent on the work being done, and there are many factors at play. Generally, the more complex the job or the bigger it is (in terms of square footage), the more the permit will cost. Depending on where you live, taxes on the material costs are often collected along with the permit fees.

Who is supposed to get the permit? The homeowner or the contractor can get the permit. Because your contractor cannot legally begin working on your home without a permit (when one is required), you should clearly define this responsibility with him. The last thing you want is for the work to be delayed because someone forgot to get the permit or thought the other person was doing it.

Either way, one thing is always true: Legal responsibility is on you, the homeowner, to ensure that you have the necessary permits and that the necessary inspections are done. Be wary if your contractor tries to convince you that a permit isn't needed. He might be right, but check, because you—not him—will be the one on the hook.

Step Five: Let the Renovation Begin—and End

By the time the work crew shows up at your door, you'll already have done a lot of work. Now the visible stuff begins. This is the part where it gets worse before it gets better—or at least gets messier before it gets cleaner. It's also where you begin to see the payoff for your careful planning: Even though some on-the-job decision-making is inevitable, your renovation is going to proceed like clockwork if you've done your work ahead of time.

In the next chapter, you'll see some advice about establishing a great working relationship with your contractor and his crew, and about making the job site—your home—a satisfactory place to be for your contractor, the crew, and your family, too.

It comes down to a solid, detailed written contract and lots of discussion with your contractor about the ins and outs of the job. This is the no-surprises way of doing things. It takes planning, not magic, to make the job run smoothly.

Taking Charge—with a Little Help

Whenever we do a TV show on a botched basement or an unfinished kitchen, we get hundreds of emails from people who had the same problem, and they all say the same thing: "I thought I was alone." That's part of the idea behind the show—to show them they're not. That's the

Will it ever end? Many people get into major renovations that seem to go on and on, with no end in sight to the disruption and mess. Living on a renovation site can be unsettling, that's for sure. In fact, I've witnessed many people divorce over the reno, which is why I sometimes call the mess "divorce dust." Having realistic expectations for how long the process will take and making sure you and your contractor agree to a schedule—in writing—should help to keep things smooth on the family front.

message I give to people when I speak at home shows. And as you start to think about renovating, that's the first thing you need to know: You are not alone. I'm here to help you.

Together we will get you through your home renovation. In fact, we'll do more than get you through it. We're going to master the process. We'll get what you want, on time, and at the right price. The right price isn't the highest, the lowest, or even the middle price. The right price is the cost of doing it right. Once. The first time.

CHAPTER TWO

Hire Right

Contractors come in threes. You've got the good, the bad, and the ugly

Let's say you want your basement redone.

You've been thinking about it for a while, and you're eager to get going. You start calling contractors, but they are all busy. They tell you it will be months before they can get to your house. You start to get desperate and forget the cardinal rule: Slow down. Finally one guy comes in, and this is your lucky day, because he can start right away—next week. He quotes a good price and then mentions that he would like 50% up front, let's say $30,000, to cover materials and to pay his crew.

Well, you're glad that he's ready to come in. But $30,000 up front like that just seems too much. So you mention this, and he immediately drops the amount to 5%. > > >

Choose the right contractor, and everything else should go fine; get it wrong and watch out

I hear stories like this all the time. I see three red flags here—those warning signs that tell you the road ahead may be rough. First, no pro can ever start tomorrow or next week. Pros are too busy. Second, pros don't need a lot of money up front; they don't live week to week. The most that contractor should have asked for is 10%, and that's only to tie up his time—to make sure he's yours and you're his. Third, that drastic drop from 50% down to 5% tells you that you're dealing with the wrong contractor. Pros don't budge. They're very kind and courteous, but the facts are the facts.

Next to you, the most important person in your renovation is the general contractor. He is the guy who will be there day in and day out. He (or she—yes, there are plenty of women working as general contractors, as well as in the trades) will be hiring and overseeing the work of the subcontractors. He will be responsible for how the work is done and when. He may bring in an architect or engineer if needed. Choose the right general contractor, and everything else should go fine; get it wrong, and watch out.

That's an obvious statement, but it is frightening how little thought most people put into finding the right contractor. When they are facing an expensive and potentially difficult task like a major renovation, most people rely on what I call the Law of Threes.

Here's how it works. Whenever I am at a home show, I'll ask people: If you are planning a renovation, how many contractors should you talk to? The answer is always the same: three. Then I'll ask: How many references should your contractor give you? Again, right across the country, three is always the No. 1 answer.

Contractors come in threes, too. You've got the good, the bad, and the ugly. The ugly are a very small group, I'd say about 10% in all. They are there to take your money and they have no conscience whatsoever. They will rob you blind. They might even take your money and never show up for the job. Or they'll show up once, remove a wall or put in a couple of studs, and never return.

The group you want are the pros. Yes, they're definitely out there. They amount to about 20% of all contractors. But they're usually booked pretty far in advance. Whether the economy is booming or struggling, good contractors are always going to be busy.

That leaves the remaining 70%, the bad. When it comes to their job, they don't know enough, or they don't

Hiring the wrong contractor leads to disaster, quickly.

BEFORE

Look what happens if you hire the wrong contractor (top two photos). In this case, a window-and-door guy got in way over his head and botched a kitchen renovation. The bottom photos are the "after" shots, once we made it right.

AFTER

care enough, or both. They practice what I call "mine over matter": It's not mine, so it doesn't matter. Most of us can spot the ugly coming from a mile away, but we're not so good at spotting the bad.

The point is, if eight out of 10 contractors don't know or don't care what they're doing, the odds against the three you've chosen to check out being among that group are pretty high. That's why it's so important to check out a lot more than three contractors—you need to make a broad slate of candidates in order to find the right one for you. And what's with this three references thing? Even the worst contractor can probably get it right three times running. Or fool three people. Three references just aren't enough.

Do You Really Need a General Contractor?

Let's take a step back and ask a different question: Do you really need a general contractor? Why not just do it yourself? After all, by some estimates you can save as much as 30% on the overall cost of the job if you don't use a general contractor. To my mind, though, unless you have unlimited time (and I really mean unlimited—you have to be there all the time) and a lot of knowledge (through courses, books, and especially hands-on experience), acting as your own general contractor is a mistake. I've said before that I'm not a big fan of DIY, and I'll say here that general contracting is not the place to make an exception. A good general contractor is a manager and an overseer, as well as (almost always) an experienced tradesman in his own right. He knows the building code, and he not only knows when permits are necessary, he also obtains those permits. The best general contractors are adept at scheduling, problem-solving, and dealing with

the unexpected. Managing large-scale renovations is a skill and an art, not to mention a full-time job. Your job is to find the right general contractor; his job is to make sure you get what you want from your renovation.

So make no mistake, you need a general contractor first and foremost. I believe that a general contractor should be hired before you think about hiring an engineer, an architect, or any other design professional. It's true that some people do go in the other direction—most often if they've discovered an architect whose work they admire and they really want to work with that person—but I recommend finding the best general contractor you can and then, if and when it's necessary, your general contractor can bring an engineer or architect onto the job. This usually eliminates unnecessary planning costs.

Let me explain. Engineers and architects are mainly

Renovating isn't like building brand new. A renovation contractor has to be skilled at tying in the old with the new. At this job, the contractor just gave up and abandoned the work.

book people. They've learned what they know in school. Most of them haven't been in the field, working. They're going to base their recommendations on numbers and calculations. You'll usually find that if you hire an architect or engineer first, they'll draw up plans; then a contractor will look at your house and at those plans or drawings and say, "This doesn't work—we're going to have to make changes." You'll have to go back to the architect to redraw the plans, and you'll wind up paying more. A good general contractor works with you and an architect or engineer—often from a list of people who work with him regularly—to come up with a workable plan that's done right the first time.

The Design Professionals: Architects, Engineers, and Interior Designers

While we're on the topic, when is the time right for an architect or engineer (or even an interior designer)? There are different ways of thinking about this. One way has to do with the cost of the project. Some people suggest that any renovation over $25,000 should have the input of a design professional. Another determining factor is the size of the space. If it's more than a few hundred square feet, for instance, they say an architect should be brought in. I don't think it's that simple. Neither cost nor size is a good indicator of whether you need or want the services of an architect. It comes down to preference, in many ways. Will you enjoy the process more if you work with an architect? You might, if the creative process is really important to you. A well-trained, experienced architect can design a beautiful space for you.

You should consider hiring an architect if you're particularly concerned about your home's style and about maintaining the integrity of that style if you're adding

Mike's TIP

What does "design-build" actually mean?

You'll sometimes see companies that describe themselves as "design-build." That's just a fancy way of saying that they offer design services along with their building services. That usually means they'll have architects or other registered designers on staff, and it's their way of setting themselves above their competitors. It can streamline the process for customers, but because you're getting so many pros in one shot, you'll want to be especially sure that you've checked out their reputations and their previous work.

What does an architect do?

Architects do more than draw pretty pictures of what your house will look like—though they do that, too. They are trained in engineering and site planning, and they understand how structures work and what they should look like—in theory, at the very least. They can create a design for your project, prepare construction (working) drawings, make sure that the plans meet minimum code, and help you estimate costs. Depending on what kind of arrangement you make with them (and how much you'll be paying them), architects can also oversee hiring a contractor and oversee the project during construction. You can pay architects in different ways: hourly, fee-for-service, or as a percentage of the whole job.

Even if you find the architect of your dreams, you don't want to hand the project over to him or her and walk away. It's still your house, and your money—you need to know what's going on at all times.

to it or changing a lot. Do you want to keep the style intact—say, for an addition to blend seamlessly with the existing house? Are you trying to restore the historical authenticity of your home, either inside or out? If any of these are concerns for you, design professionals such as architects and interior designers are essential. Although a good general contractor will have picked up a lot about good design over the years, he isn't a designer, and he may not have the expertise to help you work within a specific period style.

What about interior designers? Interior designers are more than decorators, though it's easy to see why people often get confused about this. True interior designers are registered through a professional association and are qualified to make recommendations about interior layouts, with the exception of load-bearing walls. They often pick up where architects leave off, helping you with room layouts (especially kitchens and bathrooms), space planning, and storage planning. They also help with the cosmetic choices that go into a renovation. What style of crown molding will best suit your house? What kind of cabinetry will look good in your kitchen? What kind of counters, drawer pulls, faucets, appliances? You'll be spending a lot of money on these items, and an interior designer can help you get the most bang for your buck and also save you from costly mistakes. Just as a good architect would do, a good interior designer will spend time with you finding out what you like, what your lifestyle demands, and what will best suit your needs and tastes.

Where to Look

Let's say you're looking for a general contractor to renovate your bathroom. Where do you find someone? I am leery about finding contractors through advertising, such as in the Yellow Pages. As a pro, I've never advertised in my life. Pros don't need to—word-of-mouth is their gold, how they keep going. Pros are always working and taking care of the client, never getting caught without their homework done. You're not going to find these people in the phone book. And you're probably not going to find the one right person through a real estate agent or home inspector, either, though it doesn't hurt to ask and put the names they suggest on a list of people you'll check out.

Instead, if your friends and neighbors have had a renovation and you like what you see, ask them who did it. This is really the best way—but you have to take it further. You have to go through what I'll call the dating process. When it comes to hiring someone for a renovation, you can't go with one, two, or even three possibilities—you must talk to a hundred contractors. All right, I am exaggerating. But not three. More like 20. And yes, this process will take time. But if you want a high-quality renovation that runs smoothly, on schedule, and on budget, taking time beforehand to hire the right people for the job is a step that you can't afford to skip.

The Dating Process: Interviews

When you start bringing in contractors to talk about your new bathroom, I'll tell you what you can (unfortunately) expect. You might see a guy walk in with a clipboard and say, "Uh-huh, uh-huh," when you tell him what you want. Then he's going to say, "It's going to be at least $10,000," and then he'll let you know that he doesn't want you wasting his time with questions. Now, the ballpark figure he's citing may not be unreasonable (anywhere from $10,000 to $20,000 is pretty standard for a bathroom these days), but his delivery is unacceptable. If any

If a contractor tells you to stay away from permits, stay away from that contractor

contractor talks to you like this, it's time to show him the door.

I don't really care if a guy is being called in for the smallest job, like installing bookcases or lights—I want to see him walk in with a portfolio that shows who he is and what he can do. A portfolio that says, "This is my company; my company and my employees are insured, here are my certifications, my licenses, and photos of the work I've done, and here is a full list of references." Everything should be there. The contractors with the portfolios are proud of what they do. They want you to check them out. They want you to contact other people and hear them say, "Man, this guy is good." But the ones who just say, "That'll be $10,000" or "Don't waste my time," they don't care about anything in your home, and I can't say that enough. They just don't.

▶ ▶ ▶ **If a contractor doesn't walk in with a portfolio,** a red flag should go up. Ask about it: Do you have a portfolio? Do you have a major list of references for me? And if he says, "It's a simple bathroom; what do you need references for?"—get rid of him.

▶ ▶ ▶ **You want a prospective contractor to answer your questions** and to ask a lot of his own. His first question should be, "Has anybody else done renovations here?"

From there it should be, "What are you looking for?" Anything and everything should be discussed in this first meeting, but not money—not yet. Money should be the last part of the conversation, and when it does come up, you should expect to hear an approximate cost—"You're in the $10,000 to $12,000 range," for instance—but you should also expect him to say, "I'll have to look into this in more detail before I can give you an estimate."

By asking for and expecting to see a portfolio, you will narrow down the field a lot. In fact, honestly, you may be down to one person. Because I will tell you right now, you won't get four or five guys who'll show you a portfolio. You won't, but the one who actually comes in on his own with one—he's the one you want to talk to.

Notice I said "talk." You don't want to sign right away—you want to get to know this person. Remember what I said about dating? Make this a relationship. If this were a date, would you propose marriage right away? Of course not. Finding the right contractor is no different from any other relationship in your life: You want to get to know him. Take your time on this.

And talk to him. There are questions you need to ask: How long have you been in the business? Do you specialize in one area? Have you done bathrooms and kitchens (or basements and additions)? Do you know all the aspects of renovation? (It is not the same as new-home construction.

Mike's
TIP

How long have you actually been in business?

It's not always a simple answer. Crooked contractors often operate through corporations, and to avoid liability, they change corporate names regularly. If a contractor starts a job and then disappears, the police often don't consider it fraud, but a breach of contract, a civil matter. The contractor changes his corporate name again and moves on. It's hard to hire a lawyer to take these people to court when you can't find them.

What can you do? Ask the contractor how long he has been in business and then ask how long his corporation has been around. If he's been in business for 25 years but incorporated for only one year, that's a big red flag. What did he do previously? Has he changed corporate names so he can't be sued? For a really big job, you might want to do a corporate search to double-check.

In new-home building, you must understand building theory. Renovation means having the talent to tie new work into an already existing building.) Pay attention to his responses and to what they say about his work ethic. If you ask about permits and a contractor replies that you don't need a permit for the work you want to do, that is a red flag, big-time. Most renovations will require at least one permit.

Tell the contractor what you want, but above all, learn from him while you are watching and listening for any red flags about his business or his building practices. Many people are, naturally, nervous about being in this position. When you're talking to the contractor, after all, it's his world. Where do you get off, you might wonder, talking to him about materials and techniques? Well, by the time you are ready to start talking to contractors, you will have already done a lot of work. You'll have visited the big box stores, read books and magazines, surfed the Internet, and taken seminars. You will have thought about what you want done. You'll know in general how long it should take and how much it should cost. You couldn't do it yourself, but you'll know enough to make sure someone else does it right.

A contractor's willingness (or unwillingness) to take the time to listen and explain things to you will be a sign of his personal integrity and his professionalism. A good contractor will show an interest in talking to you about what you really want, about what is feasible and what is best for you. That's the kind of contractor you want—the guy who before and during the renovation is constantly saying, "Have you thought of this? Have you looked at it this way? Here are more possibilities." And if it all seems too much, always remember one thing: It's your money, so you are the boss.

Before you hire a contractor, take a look at a few of their completed jobs

Don't just call the contractor's references. Go take a look at their work. The quality of their finishing will give you a good idea of their workmanship—and how much they care.

Checking References

The next step is to start calling the references—again, not three, but lots. When you do get hold of those other homeowners, take the opportunity to ask questions, a thousand and one questions: Did the contractor start on time? Did he finish on time? Was he courteous? Was he clean? Did he charge you money at the end of the job that you didn't expect? Did he get permits? Did he push himself to do things right? Did he educate you throughout the process, explaining what he was doing or telling you when something unexpected had happened? Did he keep you involved, or did he send you away from the job site?

Then, whenever you can, go see the contractor's work. Because if you hire this guy or this company, you are about to receive his work. If you call 20 people, try to see at least five of their actual renovations. The more you see, the better, but make sure you're specific and selective about what you see. If you're having a bathroom done, you want to see bathrooms—not decks or fences or roofs. And when you're there, ask more questions of the homeowners. Some people will speak cautiously about their contractor, even if they're on the reference list. That's a red flag. If they're not bragging to the limit, if they're not saying what a wonderful experience it was, you're likely dealing with the wrong contractor. If nobody wants you to come into their home to see a renovation, that tells you something, too. Typically, if the work is good, people are proud. When I've done bathrooms—and I've done hundreds—my clients are usually so happy and impressed that they'll almost pull people off the street to come see the work. Now, some people are very private, or they don't want to make the time to show you their place, or they worry about cleaning it up perfectly before you see it. All that aside, though, you can tell when someone is hesitating because she's not really that happy with the work. In the end, it's simple: Watch for the red flags, and trust your instincts.

The Price

I don't know if it's part of the Law of Threes, but let me tell you a third thing I always notice at home shows. I ask people: If you have three quotes—one high, one medium, and

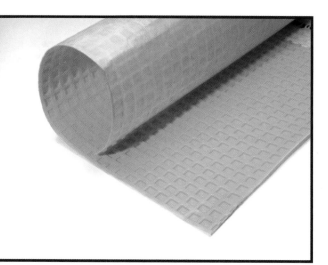

A contractor's quote should include everything required for the job, including what material, like Ditra, will be used to protect your floor tiles from cracking.

one low, which one do you go with? The answer is, invariably, the medium one. I say to them—and I am saying it to you—it has nothing to do with the price, folks. It has everything to do with what's being done and with what products.

▶ ▶ ▶ **Here's how I do a quote. As a contractor,** when I am finally sure that I know what you want and what you need, I will present a price. This price is not negotiable. I do not present you with a higher price so we can negotiate down to my real price. I give you a set price, and I do that by thinking through the project in detail—and also spelling it out in detail for you, the customer, to see.

You see, much of the time, you're going to see a quote that states the average costs for what you've asked for: a basic square-footage price for floors, basic prices for toilets, sink, tub, etc. Most contractors won't specify what type of floor tile, what type of toilet, sink, tub.

▶ ▶ ▶ **That's not good enough,** and that's not the way I do it. If I'm doing a bathroom, I'll tell you everything about those tiles: what material they are, how much grout they'll need, the type of thinset I'll use to bond the tiles

to the floor, how I'll prep the floor to prevent tiles from cracking. My quote form shows the square footage of insulation, vapor barrier, and drywall, the linear footage of trim, how many doors, doorknobs, and handles, the style and price of the faucets and shower heads—every detail is in writing. My quote also shows how many days or weeks I'll be there and how much I'll charge to clean up. I have a weekly charge for deliveries to cover running back and forth to the store. I want you to see where your money's going, in absolute detail. I've probably sold 97% of my jobs simply because I showed clients exactly where their money was going.

If people can't afford my quote, they have two options. First option: Wait, continue to save, and hopefully we can do a couple of little fix-ups to make things okay until we do the real thing the next year or two years later. Second option: Look within my quote to see if there's anything you can do without. Because everything's detailed, you can easily see what the highest-cost items are. Can you eliminate the oak trim and go to poplar or MDF? Can you replace the $285 faucets with a set worth $125? How many ceiling lights do you really need? All the wonderful extras you

wanted, they're right there in front of you. This is what you should expect from your contractor.

▶ ▶ ▶ **How can you tell if a quote is too high?** Here is a rule that may help you when looking at a quote: Generally, about 50% of the cost is going to be materials and the remaining 50% is going to be labor. If you have a very detailed quote from a contractor—one that breaks down the materials the way my quotes do—you will be able to see if the total amount (materials plus labor) makes sense. You could even do your own quote, just to get a starting point. Again with our bathroom example, tally up the cost of the materials (something you could learn by visiting a big box store and a few other places), including the tub, sink, faucets, water-resistant drywall, countertop materials, even the grout—the more specific, the better. Assume the same money again for labor, and then, just to be safe, toss in some extra on top. The closer the contractor is to this, the more likely his quote is realistic.

▶ ▶ ▶ **A detailed quote helps you in another way.** People worry about being gouged, and that's legitimate, but it's almost as bad to hire someone who quotes a price so low that he can't possibly do the job properly, or even finish it. I was on the phone with some homeowners recently who wanted to do a spa. They had two very different quotes, and they didn't know who was right. The first guy's quote was $90,000 for a 4,000-square-foot job, and he'd given the customer only a very simple list of what had to be done. I went in there and said, "You can't do it for this price!" The second guy had worked for me, and he had given details on everything in his quote. He quoted $240,000, including $115,000 in heating and materials, broken down to the last tile and faucet. If those people go with the lower quote, they're headed for trouble.

The Contract

After months of planning and talking, when it finally comes time to sign the contract, you want to see things listed in absolute detail, just as you saw on the quote. (In fact, the best thing is to attach the quote to the contract.) The contract should include the final price, any possible additional costs (more on that below), and the amount of the deposit. It should also include a warranty that states when the work will start and when it is to be finished.

▶ ▶ ▶ **The contract will set out payment terms.** One reason people stay involved with a bad contractor and don't pull the plug is that they've given the contractor a large down payment and they've ended up caught in a financial trap. You hear this: "Well, we've already given him $30,000, so we've got to deal with him." Avoid this situation by paying a deposit to the contractor at the beginning (no more than 10%), then paying set amounts at predetermined milestones—after the framing is done,

or the plumbing rough-in, for instance. This means that you've never put out money for work that hasn't been done. If anything goes wrong, nobody really loses.

If it were up to me, I would also add incentive and penalty clauses. Homeowners who are smart with their money will add a penalty clause that states something like this: If the job is not fully completed on schedule, we'll deduct $1,000 a week, because now you're costing us time. Pros will accept this challenge because they're almost always on time (unless a homeowner starts asking for changes midway through a job). To balance the penalty clause, you can build in incentives. If the contractor is done on time, for instance, you agree to pay a bonus of $1,000. An agreement like this works for both homeowners and contractors. If the guy's good, he'll win that $1,000. However, never make the penalty or incentive too big— that can cause arguments, and we never want to argue.

▶ ▶ ▶ **I suggest the following rule (my friends call it Holmes's Law): Never give a contractor more than what was in the contract.** But how can you avoid those extra thousands being added on to your final bill? The main thing is to make sure the contract spells everything out clearly—including any possible additional costs. You don't want to hear rationalizations like, "Oh, we didn't know the HVAC was in the wall." Pros have a pretty good idea what's in the wall, though they may not always know what condition it will be in, or what exactly will be required to replace or work around it. With the knowledge they have, they can build in a list of possible "surprises." And that's why they should always ask you about any previous renovations—it prepares them for some of the surprises they might uncover. The more that is included in the possibilities list of the contract, the more comfortable

CONTRACT

I know some homeowners who've agreed to a home renovation project with just a handshake. Don't do it. No matter what size your project is, you need a contract.

Educate yourself and control what happens. Don't just sign the contract the contractor hands you—read it, and if you don't like it, change it. You can delete and add comments or draw up your own contract for the contractor to sign.

A good contract is easy to read, detailed, no-nonsense, and include at least these points:

WHO ARE YOU CONTRACTING WITH?

Make sure you understand who you're doing business with. If the name on the contract is not the person you've been dealing with, ask why. If it is a company, find out how long it's been in business. If it's new, or if it's one of several companies the contractor uses, these are red flags.

DETAILED QUOTE

A good contractor will give you a precise quote, listing details about work to be done, materials to be used, and time to complete the job in writing. That quote should be attached to the agreement, and the contractor should agree to do the work precisely as set out in the quote. It should include time and cost for obtaining permits, if the contractor is getting them.

CHANGE ORDERS

Even a great contractor may not be able to predict everything that can occur once the job starts. The quote should contain potential problems that could arise, and it should state clearly that all changes to the contract must first be agreed to in writing. If you request a change that involves additional material or labor, there must be a change order specifying the change and the cost signed by you and by the contractor.

START AND FINISH DATES

Good contractors should start on time and should be able to tell, within reason, how long a job will take. The contract should also set out what might delay the start or completion. For instance, work can be delayed by architects and engineers revising plans, permit issues, or even weather.

INCENTIVES AND PENALTY CLAUSES

To ensure the job starts and runs on time, you can add incentives and penalties. Maybe you can agree that if the contractor finishes on time, you'll pay a bonus of $1,000 and that for each week past the finish date, you can dock the contractor $1,000 off the final payment.

PAYMENT SCHEDULE

Payment must be based on milestones in the work. It starts with the down payment, which should be no more than 10%, up to $2,500 maximum. Never pay a contractor more unless your job requires custom materials. Often, custom work requires materials that may be a significant out-of-pocket expense for the contractor and are unlikely to be used on another job.

The contract should then set out payments as the work is completed. Always keep the payments balanced with the completed work. Pay 10% when the job starts, 10% when framing is up and passed, 10% on completion and inspection of electrical and plumbing rough-in, etc. The final payment must not be paid until all the work is done to your satisfaction.

SUBCONTRACTORS

Contracts must say if all subcontractors are licensed, certified and the contractor will pay them. It should say that prior to each payment date, the contractor must let you know which subcontractors have worked and give you a letter from each indicating that they have been paid. If they have not, you can ensure they get paid.

TERMINATION CLAUSE

Contracts should include reasons that give you the right to terminate without any claim by the contractor. Some reasons are if the job starts very late, runs significantly late, if work is not being done to building code, if the contractor is not using materials listed in the quote, if subcontractors aren't being paid, or if the work site is frequently unsafe.

What about those permits?

Prior to construction—or even demolition—you or your contractor must obtain all the necessary permits to do the job. Those permits should be posted in a window on the job site. Later, when the work is completed, keep all permits and inspection reports for your records. Never get rid of permits! They are like a map to your home, providing solid proof of what's been done, and where. They're important for you, and for the resale value of your home.

the homeowner should be. If there's no list of possible problems, well, that's all right, but it's not ideal—a good contractor will expect a few surprises. At the end of the job, make sure that if the problem didn't come up, you don't pay for it.

► ► ► **In the same spirit, the contract should make it clear that if the homeowner wants a change** not included in the original estimate, that costs the contractor extra time and money. Some of the biggest complaints I hear from contractors have to do with homeowners who change their minds on an almost daily basis. Of course, you can change your mind, but you must understand that it is always going to cost you. And it may not be great for the relationship you have with your contractor—you may be wreaking havoc with his schedule, including the jobs he's promised to other clients. Here's what I do: For every change to what we originally contracted, I create a change order. It gives details about what the customer wants to change, the cost of the change, and the estimated change to the job's completion date. The change order becomes part of the contract, signed and dated by both the contractor and the client. This means no surprises at the end of the project. Keep it fair and clear,

and you'll have a great relationship with your contractor.

Most people assume that a contract is needed only in case you ever end up in court. That's not the way I see it at all. You don't want to go to court, and having a thorough contract from the beginning will help you avoid it. The contract is something like a promissory note: It states exactly what the contractor intends to do and for how much—I promise to start on this date, I promise to finish on this date, I will use the materials and techniques listed in detail in the attached quote. As long as you have everything spelled out, there's no room for argument between the two of you. You need to talk about how changes will be handled once the work starts and, more important, what will happen if there is a dispute or you are unhappy with how the work is proceeding. A detailed contract eliminates surprises. For both you and your contractor, it ensures job satisfaction.

Before the Work Begins

From the beginning, you want to make sure that your relationship with your contractor is a good one. Like any good relationship, it's about mutual respect. You don't have to become best buddies with your contractor, but the fact is that your contractor and his crew are going to

A cleaner job site is a safer one

A good contractor keeps his job site (which is also your home) clean and the mess contained. It's more than just common courtesy; a clean site is safer for everyone. In the top photo, the contractor used plastic sheeting to contain the dust in the part of the house that was under renovation.

Mike's TIP

Getting along with the second-most important person

You've probably heard lots of warnings about how to get along with your contractor. Don't be too nosy, don't ask too many questions, don't make any suggestions—right? Wrong. A good contractor doesn't mind an owner asking questions. In fact, a good contractor loves to teach, and is always looking for opportunities to let you know how your house works and how his work is going to improve your home. Of course, you should show respect for your contractor's knowledge and experience, and of course you should be wary of spending too much of his time in conversation. But remember: it's your house, and your money. It's your right to know.

become part of your home life for the duration of your renovation, so it's worth the effort to get along.

A good relationship means that, after you've set a start date but before work begins, you establish ground rules and expectations—what time the workers can come into your house in the morning, where they should park, where they should eat while they're in your house, which bathroom they should use (although a portable toilet might be a smart investment), what they should do with their garbage at the end of the day, etc. You should discuss which parts of the house will have to be cleared out while the renovations are happening, and make sure you have this done well before the workers arrive on the first day. Talk about where the workers will place plastic door coverings, and about which floors, if any, need to be protected with a thick layer of paper before the demolition work begins. If you work from a home office, will you be able to function normally? Will their music bother you (or vice versa)? A good relationship means you'll get the best work out of a very skilled bunch of men and women, and you'll enjoy being around when the work is happening. A bad relationship could mean that you end up with a skunk or old sandwiches in the wall because the workers don't care about you anymore (and believe me, I have found lots worse).

On the Job

As the work begins, you'll need to find the right balance between being there to answer questions as they come up and giving your contractor enough freedom to work quickly and without disruption. In my view, it's always good to generally stick around, to check in at least once a day, and to be easily reachable by phone. Most people want to avoid the dust and the rubble and the craziness that comes with their renovation; sometimes they even go on vacation to get away from it all. I don't recommend that. This is your house, and you need to be involved. As your contractor works, you must ask questions and learn what he and his crew are doing. Believe me, if you're respectful in how you ask, the pros won't mind, because they want you to know why they're doing what they're doing.

Renovations, by their nature, involve lots of decision-making along the way, even with the best of planning ahead of time. Lots of conversations will happen, and lots of minor decisions will be made as you go. A good idea is to keep a notebook handy and record all those minor decisions, so that you can protect yourself from any arguments later about who agreed to do what. If it's a major change, of course, a change order will be needed, but for many smaller items (a change of paint color, for instance, or a different color of grout for the bathroom tile), making notes in a book that both you and your contractor can consult could save a lot of trouble later on.

Here's another major piece of insurance: Take pictures—before, during, and after your renovation. Take pictures of absolutely everything: how the plumbing and electrical work were completed, the framing, the insulation, the floors as they were being installed. The more pictures you take, the more it will work for you in the future. If ever there's a problem, you can show it to another pro. If you ever want to sell your home, photographs provide evidence of what's been done behind the drywall. And they may come in handy if you have trouble. Don't forget to keep copies of the building inspections, too.

Spotting the Red Flags

How can you spot trouble? And when it hits the fan,

how can you deal with it? If you know about red flags, if you watch for them, and if you act when you see them, you can probably avoid serious trouble, or at least nip it before it goes too far.

Earlier in this chapter, I mentioned some of the red flags to watch out for with a contractor: being too readily available, asking for too much money up front, budging too easily on terms, trying to work without the necessary permits. Here are some others.

▶ ▶ ▶ **Delays.** You may have been told that the work would begin on June 8. Instead, the month of June and almost the entire month of July have gone by before the crew arrives for even one day of work. When they finally do get there on July 30, you hear something like this: "I'm sorry, we've been really busy, blah, blah, blah." Pros are always—always—on time. If nothing else, they will come in on the first scheduled day and at least start to keep their word. That's the difference between someone with integrity and someone who doesn't care about you. The guy with integrity feels he must stand behind what he says. The other guy's attitude could be summed up like this: You'll wait for me because just try to find someone else. Or maybe they're taking too long to finish the job. You scheduled start and finish times before you started, so why are they taking forever? Pros know how long it's going to take, and usually they are correct. If a contractor doesn't do what he says he's going to do from the beginning, that's a huge red flag.

▶ ▶ ▶ **Excuses.** Let's say your contractor and his crew didn't show up for two consecutive days, and he didn't call you. "Well, my truck broke down," he tells you afterwards, or "My supplier didn't deliver the drywall." Few of us will argue when we hear things like that; we automatically say, "Oh, by all means, go do what you've got to do." After all, it could be a real emergency. But in most cases, the contractor was actually trying to finish another job. He had an irate client and he's tried to solve that by squeezing out of his work for you. If a contractor is going to miss a day (and yes, things do come up), he should let you know the day before. If the excuses continue, that is a big red flag.

▶ ▶ ▶ **Messy job sites and other dangerous habits.** If the job site is dirty, you have a bad contractor, guaranteed. Pros keep their job sites clean. On any job, cleanliness is a safety issue. But if he's a messy contractor, he obviously doesn't care about safety, and that's important for you to know. It's a danger sign, too, if he's renting tools from a huge rental company. Pros don't rent tools. They own them. And pros especially don't ask to borrow your tools.

Look for these signs. Trust these signs. If you see them, take action immediately. Do not play around, because if you have problems at the beginning, just wait until the end—you've seen nothing yet. Unless you do something, it can only get worse.

So what should you do? If you have a well-written contract, I suggest a "three strikes and you're out" policy.

▶ ▶ ▶ **1. Speak to your contractor.** You should raise your concerns only with your contractor, especially if you have a problem with one of the subcontractors. Be reasonable and listen carefully to his explanations. Be sure to document your conversation, including his explanation.

▶ ▶ ▶ **2. If that fails, put your concerns in writing.** In your letter, clearly describe the problems and give the contractor a set time to solve them. If your concerns fall into the group that allows you to terminate your contract, let him know, in writing, that if he misses the deadline, you will hire another contractor to finish the work, using money remaining from your contract. Once your contractor has read the letter, ask him to initial your copy of it.

▶ ▶ ▶ **3. If you're still not happy after your deadline passes,** and if your concerns do allow you to terminate the contract, tell your contractor to go immediately. You will probably need to speak to a lawyer about whether your concerns are serious enough to justify immediate termination. That is why a good contract is very important—if the list of potential problems permitting termination has been given enough thought, you can avoid involving costly lawyers.

This may seem tough. But remember: You're the boss. You're paying for it, it's your home, and you must maintain that power. Don't take advantage of your position and yell and scream, but be firm and take no excuses. Tell him to go.

In some cases, the contractor who is fired may be open to ending the relationship and you can make an amicable financial settlement—that is, one in which you pay only for work already completed. But if you do fire your contractor,

A good relationship means that, after you've set a start date but before work begins, you establish ground rules and expectations

other problems may well come up. Kick them off the job site before the job is finished, and some contractors will threaten to put a lien on your house (this means to stake a legal claim to it until they've been paid), and they actually have a legal right to do that.

A whole book could be written about residential construction contracts in the United States, and many chapters would be given over to liens and the rights of contractors, subcontractors and homeowners. No two states' lien laws are the same; that's why things can get so complicated.

If a contractor or subcontractor places a lien on your house, you won't be able to sell or mortgage it until the debt has been paid. Liens are designed to protect contractors who did not get paid by homeowners. They are also designed to protect subcontractors. Because construction lien laws are designed to protect contractors and subcontractors, those are the only people they usually protect—not you. Even if the reason you refuse to pay is that the work is incomplete or not done properly, the contractor can come after you with a construction lien. However, contractors and subcontractors can put a lien on

your house only within a certain time limit, which varies from state to state.

If there is a lien put on your house, don't panic. Don't react in fear and certainly don't pay money right away. Just because there is a lien on the house, sometimes for a lot of money, it doesn't mean you owe all the money or that the contractor who put the lien on your home can have the house sold. Sometimes the lien is justified, but more often than not the contractor is angry and trying to get revenge by causing you some frustration or simply trying to squeeze money out of you. You will have a chance to defend yourself and fight the lien if that is appropriate. So, the first thing to do is calm down. Then find out the facts if you don't already know them. Once you know more facts, you can begin to think about how to respond and consult with a lawyer if necessary.

If you have to fight the lien, can you win? If you've protected yourself with a contract, if you were careful from the beginning about getting everything possible in writing, if you took pictures of your home before, during, and after the renovation, you will be relatively safe. If you don't have documentation and you end up in court, the

Thoroughly checking out the contractor <u>before</u> you sign a contract is the one thing that's going to save you

contractor might win. Why? Because if you don't have documents that prove what the contractor was supposed to do, it becomes your word against his or hers. And if the contractor comes across like a pro and you do not, odds are you'll lose. Also, if you don't have the documents you should to bolster your position, it's a lot more likely that you'll need to hire another general contractor or engineer to help you in court. They can say what it is that your contractor should have done at your home if the work is sloppy, but they can never say what the original deal was. For that you have to have a contract, and if you find yourself in court without one, you messed up.

Some people who have been burned by a contractor (let's say he has taken their money and just stopped showing up) think they can go to court and get their money back. It's difficult and I can only wish them luck—or you, if you choose to go this route. Just try to find the contractor and get him into court—you'll see what a battle it's going to be. Think the legal system is going to save you? It's more likely to do the opposite. It could cost you thousands of dollars, misery, and headaches, and even if you do eventually win your case, you may never be able to collect the money. I can't tell you how many cases I've

seen where the homeowners never got a dollar. When they go to court they are thrilled and happy if they win the case. Then they ask the contractor for the money and he ignores them. After asking a few more times—and being ignored—they realize they have to use a lawyer to get the contractor to reveal his assets, which will involve, more likely than not, more legal fees.

In other cases, where homeowners do get a judgment against the contractor, they discover that the contractor has no assets. He or she may live in a great house, but their partner owns it. They spend more time and money only to find that all the cars he or she drives are leased. I could go on with these examples, but take my word for it—in most cases, you really do not want to go to court.

That brings us right back to how important it is to deal with the right people. Thoroughly checking out the general contractor before you sign the contract is the one thing that's going to save you. I can't say it enough: Take the time to educate yourself and find the right contractor.

The goal. A quality renovation, on time and on budget, isn't impossible if you hire right.

CHAPTER THREE
Inside Your House 101

Too often when we think about renovating, we focus only on the finishing

The cracks in the tile were the giveaway. As I walked into the fantastic-looking bathroom, those cracks were the first thing I noticed. As always in renovating, one thing led to another. One crack in the marble floor tile near the tub, and another at the base of the shower, led us to mold behind the tiles and to water-saturated drywall. The more we looked, the worse it got. The tub drained slowly because it wasn't vented properly. The bathtub drain and the shower both leaked—in fact, the only reason the kitchen below wasn't full of water was that the guys who had done the job had left so much rubble between the floors: The water was being absorbed by the rubble. We found dangerous wiring. And we found the reason for the cracks: The floor joists were hacked up so badly they were structurally compromised. I told the homeowners I was surprised the tub hadn't fallen through the floor. All this from two fairly small cracks. > > >

Too often when we think about renovating, we focus only on the finishing, the surfaces—the marble tile, the new cabinets, or the fancy trim. That stuff is great—in fact, those choices are among the most exciting parts of home renovating, and it's those finishing touches that we come to love about our homes—but we need to look beyond and behind all that if we are going to do a job properly and spend money wisely.

▶ ▶ ▶ **Whether you're thinking of buying a home that you want to renovate** or you want to renovate the house you already own, you need to understand your home. Yes, you need to know your home before you bring in a contractor and start making changes, because only then can you talk to a contractor about it intelligently. It's your home—and your investment—to protect and make the most of.

As well as fixing up many houses over the years, I have done many, many home inspections for people who were thinking of buying a home or planning a renovation. That's what we're going to do now. I am going to walk you through your home and show it to you as you've probably never seen it before. I'll show you how to look at it from bottom to top, from inside out. I'll tell you what to look for and what you can expect a contractor to tell you. Take this book and carry it with you through your own home. And if you see things that seem bad, don't worry. Remember that everything—and I mean everything—can be fixed.

▶ ▶ ▶ **Any contractor or house inspector will talk about "code," or building code,** when inspecting, renovating, or building a house. Very simply, the building code (and the electrical and plumbing codes) ensures that houses meet a minimum standard. Codes are fairly uniform across the

United States, but there are lots of regional differences too. As recently as 100 years ago, there wasn't really any type of building code. Families got together, built each other's homes, and helped each other out; tradesmen had time and cared about what they did. But building practices have changed, and even with building codes, we're building worse and worse. Why? Because building to code is only the bare minimum. It's the worst that you're allowed to build legally. Assuming the unexpected doesn't happen, your house won't fall down, blow down, or leak, the electrical system should be fine, and the plumbing system will be right. It's like building a little car with tiny tires, a tiny engine, and the bare minimum of safety features. It will be roadworthy, but if you get into an accident, you're on your own. When you're inspecting your home, code is the starting point, but it is only the minimum. As you embark on a renovation project, always do better than minimum code.

Inspecting the Basement and Foundation

The first area we want to see is always the basement. That is No. 1 in any building inspection because it allows us to examine the foundation.

First, let's look at what foundations do and how they work. Foundation walls rest on footings, which are about twice the width of the wall itself. The footings, in turn, rest—or should rest—on undisturbed earth. When builders dig a foundation, they're trying to accomplish several things. In colder parts of the continent, they want to create a warm area under the house to keep the main living spaces warmer. They also want to dig down far enough that frost's heaving and thawing won't affect the house too much. In northern parts of the country,

Poured concrete foundations are common for renovations and new homes

Poured concrete foundations (top) are a popular choice, but contractors need to make sure that the concrete cures properly (bottom), since curing too quickly will affect its strength.

this means digging at least four feet below grade ("grade" is surface level). The minimum depth is 12 inches below grade in areas with no frost (southern states) and can be deeper.

Finally, they want to take advantage of millions of years of natural compaction by digging down to earth that has not been previously dug up and tamped down. If they don't do this, there may be problems with shifting. The foundation has to support the weight of the house, but it also has to hold up against the pressure of the earth around it; if a foundation is going to shift, that pressure is what will cause it. Some old homes—at least 100 years old— may not have been built on footings, or the ground on which they were constructed may have been disturbed. In those cases, shifting will already have occurred many years ago, and there is usually no concern about further shifting.

▶▶▶ **I've seen a lot of basements where the structure has been compromised,** either by another contractor or by a homeowner who has made adjustments on his own. Where it hasn't been done right, it can cause troubles. I have walked into basements that were literally leaning

in by eight inches—at that point, the foundation is barely holding anything up. The worst case I ever saw was a cinder-block (now known as concrete blocks or even concrete masonry units) foundation where someone had dug down and cut through the foundation wall to put in a door to the basement. When they dug down and put in concrete block for the walkout, they didn't waterproof the foundation properly, and they compacted the dirt when they pushed the wall back in. Then, when water got into the new foundation, it froze and pushed the wall inward so much that the house needed to be supported temporarily until a new foundation wall could be put in. Doing something wrong in the first place—even something so minor—can cause a catastrophe of financial issues and headaches down the road.

If this scares you, it shouldn't, because even a foundation can be fixed. It seldom costs as much money as people think to jack up a house and put in a new foundation. As long as there is room for the contractors to access the outside of your house, it's going to cost in the area of $30,000 to $50,000, and if you have a great old house in a location that you love, the

investment could be worth it.

When I look at a basement, I always hope to find it unfinished (that is, without drywalled ceilings and walls) because I want to be able to see the foundation walls, along with the many other workings of a house that are visible only in an unfinished basement. Even if the basement is finished, there is usually at least one place where I can see the foundation, and that is the utility room (furnace room, though water heaters, washers and dryers are also sometimes found here).

▶▶▶ **The first big question when examining the foundation has to do with moisture.** When you look at the walls, do you see efflorescence—a white, salty, crystalline deposit? If you see efflorescence, you know that the wall is getting wet on the outside, wicking moisture right through, and leaving the salts on the inside of the wall. If your basement is finished and you can't see the foundation walls, there are other ways you can look for signs of moisture. A musty smell, for instance, usually indicates that moisture is trapped somewhere. Look at the base of the drywall: Has it deteriorated? Does it have surface mold? If you see water stains or mold, check to see if there is a downspout outside your house at that point. That may be the offender.

▶ ▶ ▶ **Why so much concern about moisture?** Well, unchecked moisture leads to a raft of long-term, chronic problems, including mold (which can make you or your family sick) and rot in your foundation or even in the wooden components of your house's structure. Insects can be a problem, too. What do insects love to live in? Spiders, cockroaches, and especially carpenter ants all love rotted wood. If flooding occurs, you have shorter-term—but equally devastating—problems, such as damaged possessions and a destroyed furnace or appliances. We want, always, to keep out moisture, whether or not we plan to renovate the basement. And we can do this, usually by working from the outside. Throughout this chapter, I'll talk

about what you can do to make your basement moisture-free.

The second question to ask about foundations is what kind of foundation the house rests on. The answer to this question tells us a few things. First, it usually indicates the approximate age of the house, since building practices have changed over time. Second, it may tell us how well supported the house is. Finally, the type of foundation tells us how likely it is that moisture is getting through. Your house may have a foundation

of fieldstone, brick, concrete block, poured concrete, or insulated concrete forms (ICFs). Each has its pros and cons.

Fieldstone basements indicate a house that is usually over 100 years old. They are constructed of rocks (fieldstones) held together with mortar. These foundations are very thick, up to 32 inches. At that time, there was no technology for making the wall waterproof on the outside, so foundations were designed with the expectation that water would dissipate as it worked

Efflorescence, the white, salty, crystalline deposit on the right, is a sign that moisture is getting through your foundation wall.

Insulated concrete forms (ICF) provide strength and insulation

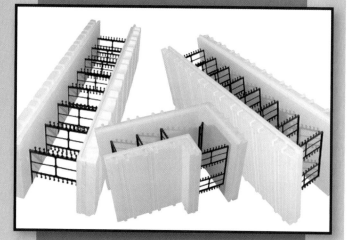

Insulated concrete forms, known as ICFs, are my ideal choice for building a new or replacement foundation. Rigid foam blocks (top photo) are fitted together like Lego, and then concrete is poured into the hollow centers (bottom photo). The wall is perfectly straight, doesn't need a vapor barrier, and has an insulation rating of R-40.

its way through the thick walls. Areas with a high water table may show greater than usual deterioration in fieldstone foundations. What can a homeowner with a stone or fieldstone foundation do? First of all, it's not recommended to finish your basement if you have this type of foundation, and odds are you only have a crawl space. If you need to repair a fieldstone foundation, it may make more sense to jack up your house and replace the foundation.

I have occasionally seen homes with brick foundations, but these are uncommon. Brick foundations suffer from one major drawback: The clay used to make bricks is highly absorbent. Brick foundations are also more vulnerable to shifting because of the number of bricks you need to use and the high ratio of mortar to solid brick.

After stone foundation walls, we really started to get into concrete foundations. Believe it or not, these were first made by actually putting in a form and pouring into it some handmade concrete that was mixed up in a wheelbarrow. After that, concrete blocks became a popular choice for building foundations because they were a lot faster and easier. This was the first step on the way to modern concrete basements. Concrete-block basements can be fine. They aren't as strong as poured-concrete basements, because some of them don't contain the stone found in concrete, but they are fairly durable. Again, like bricks, concrete blocks absorb water. Normally they were installed with a waterproof parge coating on the exterior, but in my experience this never completely covers them and some water will work its way into the basement. Also, parging is prone to cracking and heaving over the years, especially as water works its way into small fissures and frost takes its inevitable toll.

A conventional poured-concrete foundation is good if it is done right—and if it is insulated on the outside with 2 inches of vapor-impermeable rigid foam, which is done today but was not done 20 years ago. The foam acts as a vapor barrier and as insulation.

▶ ▶ ▶ **It's common for new houses to have poured concrete basements,** but unfortunately, in many cases, the concrete has not been poured properly. Either the contractors are adding more water than they should when the concrete is being mixed, they are pouring it in cold weather, or they are letting the sun get to it before it has hardened, technically known as curing. Why? Because people are impatient. Whatever the particulars, in many cases the concrete is not curing properly, and this is affecting its strength. We're seeing cracking and spalling—where the concrete actually starts to flake off. You can fix cracks in a poured foundation if you hire a hydraulic injection company. They will come in and do a series of core holes within that crack, they'll pin it, and they'll inject concrete into the holes. Normally they'll guarantee their work for five to 10 years.

▶ ▶ ▶ **Precast concrete sections are another popular method** for building a foundation today. Contractors like them because they let them put in a foundation very quickly. All in all, these foundations work well structurally. However, if they are leaking or there are signs of moisture, they will need to be fixed. You'll have to dig down to the footings around the outside perimeter. At the minimum, use an asphalt coating, then a dimpled black plastic material, preferably with fabric on the outside. The dimples allow the wall to breathe, and the fabric will wick any moisture right down to your perforated pipe and away from your foundation.

My ideal foundation, either for a new house or as a replacement foundation (when that's possible), uses ICFs. These forms are made of rigid foam with hollow centers, and essentially fit together like Legos (there are even lots of different sizes and configurations available, just like Legos). They are reinforced with rebar, and then concrete is poured into the hollow centers, creating a perfectly straight wall insulated with a built-in vapor barrier for an insulation value of up to R-40. On the outside, there should be an added layer of moisture protection: a seamless, rubberized, spray-on foundation coating. When the coating is dry, it resembles an enormous elastic band wrapped around the foundation of the house. It can stretch and move with the structure, it is waterproof, and although it's more expensive than other methods of sealing your foundation, it's well worth it.

▶ ▶ ▶ **While we're down in the basement, we need to check more than just the foundation walls**—we also need to check the floors. If they are poured concrete, that's wonderful. But if the concrete is painted, that can be a cause for worry. Paint may be trapping moisture in the concrete, and we don't want to do that. We want the concrete to breathe. Another cause for concern is linoleum or vinyl flooring, because these are stuck down using a mastic that mold loves. If the basement gets wet, mold is going to thrive under the vinyl.

Something else to check are the wooden joists that support the floors above the basement. In a basement with an unfinished ceiling, it's easy to see them: They are the long wooden pieces that run either the length or the width of your house, on the underside of the main floor. At one time in building history, joists were made from 2 x 10s, but 2 x 8s are more common now. Joists are typically set 16 inches apart, braced every 4 feet, and need to be doubled up around stairwells and other openings in the floor to give extra structural strength. Cracking tile and grout led many builders today to put in 2 x 8 joists with 12" centers (the distance from the middle of one joist to the middle of the next joist) to beef up their floors for tiles. It would be better if the joists were 2 x 10 or 2 x 12. But if you're using manufactured floor joists, which I really like, minimum

code allows them to be placed on 19 ⅜ centers, the equivalent of three joists every 48 inches. Even if you are using manufactured floor joists, the ideal is placing your joists on 12" centers, braced every 4 feet. I know they say you don't have to, but the more we brace our floors, the more uniform and tight we make it. It's not a lot of money, it's not a lot of work, and it's the best your floor can be.

Aside from determining how far apart the joists are (and closer is better), you want to see if anyone has fooled with them over the years—hacking through them, for example. Although the building code allows for some wiring and plumbing to be run through joists (which requires making small holes through a series of joists), making substantial cuts in joists is a real no-no: It severely compromises the structural support that joists can give.

Inspect the subfloor from underneath and see how many nails have missed the floor joists. Every nail that misses a floor joist allows for more movement in the floor between joists, which creates a more bouncy floor and is also a sign of poor workmanship.

Crawl Spaces and Slabs

Particularly if you live in one of the warmer parts of North America, your home may not have a basement. Instead, it will have either a slab foundation or a crawl space—a space anywhere from 2 to 5 feet high.

A slab foundation is, as its name suggests, a very thick slab of concrete poured directly onto undisturbed soil. If your house was built on slab, the structure is more than likely fine. But problems could lie underneath it. Is the slab foundation insulated, and how? I hope it has drainage stone and then a 2-inch layer of rigid foam topped with 4 to 6 inches of 3500 PSI concrete. If you don't have

Attaching a subfloor to floor joists. Building code allows floor joists to be spaced 16" apart, while manufactured floor joists (above) are permitted to be 19 ³/8" apart. My ideal is putting your floor joists only 12" apart. You'll have a stronger, quieter floor.

What's mold got to do with it?
THE HEALTHY HOUSE

We're hearing a lot about mold these days. That's not surprising. Modern building trends have two fatal flaws when it comes to mold: Houses are being sealed too tightly and not ventilated adequately, and builders are rushing to get the job done as quickly as possible. Mold can start before the new owners even move in.

Mold thrives wherever there is moisture and lack of air movement. The space between the walls of a really tightly sealed modern house provides the perfect environment. But why would that space be wet to begin with, if the house is supposed to be so tightly sealed?

First of all, you can't assume the house is waterproof from the outside just because it was sealed with house wrap. If the seams and any holes weren't taped, or if the wrap wasn't handled properly around windows or doors, moisture can get in. And if water isn't properly carried away from the foundation walls, it can infiltrate through the basement.

Even if water can't get in from the outside, the lumber for the stud walls might have been wet when the house was built and closed in. Or moisture from inside the house, especially in the bathroom or kitchen, can get into the walls.

Why worry about mold? Well, mold literally lives off the cellulose in your home's wood studs—that's right, the studs that hold up your entire house. If mold eats at them long enough, it can compromise the actual structure. And some types of mold can be toxic, causing you or your family to a whole raft of health problems.

What to do? If you are looking at buying a new house, you really don't have any way of knowing if there is an existing or potential mold problem. You can check for the obvious things—adequate ventilation in the kitchen and bathrooms, proper grading away from the foundation—but you can't see any holes or untaped seams in the house wrap once the siding is on.

A renovation, however, is your chance to make your house mold-free. Proper

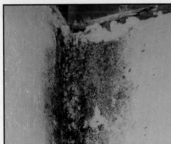

Where there's moisture, there's mold. Not only can moisture that seeps into your home cause rot and degrade finished surfaces, it's also the perfect medium for the growth of harmful, potentially fatal molds.

venting (which includes high-quality fans and/ or sufficient air vents), especially in the kitchen, bathrooms, laundry room, and attic, will help move moist air out of the house. A good vapor barrier and mold-resistant drywall and paint will also help, especially in those rooms with moisture-laden air. If you are doing work with the exterior walls, make sure they are well sealed against water infiltration, especially around doors and windows. If your house is brick veneer, be especially aware of the risk that rainwater can get

through the brick and then not drain out fast enough, or at all. If you are working on the basement, watch for signs that moisture is working its way through the foundation. Make sure your gutters and drainpipes are tight and taking water well away from the foundation. And, ideally, the foundation walls should be sealed from the outside.

Is it really worth taking so many precautions against mold? Absolutely. It's not just your biggest investment that's at risk—it's potentially the health of you and your family.

insulation, the floor will can allow moisture to travel up through it.

With a crawl space, the mechanical systems of the house, including wiring and plumbing (where the crawl space is insulated), can be installed away from the main living area. Often uninsulated, crawl spaces can have a dirt, gravel, or concrete floor. Trying to heat a house built over an uninsulated area is tough. In my part of the continent (the Great Lakes area of Canada), I would generally tell people to stay away from such homes, but I know that is not always possible. So, if your house has an uninsulated crawl space under it, what is the best thing to do?

You have two options. As built, your crawl space is a cold zone; the rest of your home (everywhere that's insulated) is a warm zone. One solution would be to convert the crawl space under your home into a warm zone. To do this, you need to insulate the walls and then put down some sort of vapor barrier on the floor. Ideally, this would be rigid foam insulation over gravel. This will stop moisture from coming up and keep the area warm. You must have a heating duct to allow heat into that space, and a cold air return down there, too, to balance out the air exchange to and from that area.

The other option is to make the crawl space into a proper cold zone—one that doesn't leach heat from the underside of your house or bring more moisture problems. To do this, you must have ventilation and insulation. A good rule is that you need one square foot of ventilation for every 150 square feet of crawl space and there must be one vent within three feet of each corner of the crawl space.

▶ ▶ ▶ **Insulation is needed to protect the warm zones of your house,** which means insulating under the floor of

your home. This would generally be batt insulation, pushed up between the joists. But you would need something to hold it there, perhaps metal mesh or, better, a breathable construction paper such as Tyvek or Typar. Spray-on foam insulation is getting to be a popular choice, too. I remember a job I did way up north, insulating the floor in a house that was just freezing. The crawl space was maybe 18 inches high, and I didn't have a lot of room to move. There were spiders galore and pretty well every other creature that lives in the earth—not an area you want to be in!

HVAC (Heating, Ventilation, and Air Conditioning)

Your home inspection continues where we'll find the heating, ventilation, and air-conditioning systems of your house. Taken together, these are sometimes referred to as HVAC. Your furnace—which will tell us both how the air in your home is heated or cooled and how the air moves through your house—likely dominates your utility room, or one corner of your basement, although the best spot for your furnace for even airflow is in the center of the house. Let's look at what you might find there.

FORCED AIR

The most common heating system in most houses, new or old, is forced air. In forced air systems, air is heated within the furnace and then forced through ducts enclosed in the walls of the house or between the floor joists to the different rooms. The outlets for the ducts are located in the floor or low on the walls in the rooms of your home. Unheated air is brought back to your furnace for heating via a cold air return, which is typically a large grate in the floor or close to the ceiling, that opens up to another type of duct. The furnace draws in air through the cold air return, filters and warms it up, then pumps it out again. It is a constant circular motion, and it's critical that the amount of hot air being forced through is equal to the amount of cold air being returned to the furnace.

► ► ► Forced air systems are usually fueled by natural gas, but they can also run off oil, electricity, or propane—even coal or wood. These various fuel sources have their pros and cons. Costs vary, as do the environmental impacts of each. If your furnace is old enough to consider replacing, you'll want to check into the facts for each fuel source before you decide. I'll get back to the topic of new furnaces in a few paragraphs.

One nice thing about forced air is that you can attach a humidifier to the furnace to pump moisture through the house along with the warm air. This will keep the house from getting too dry in the winter. And here is another of forced air's great pluses: The ducts that carry heat from the furnace can be used to blast out cool air in the summer if you install central air conditioning. Also, a forced air system allows you to connect a heat-recovery ventilation unit (HRV), which may be required by minimum code in your area. An HRV does two things: It brings fresh air in to the furnace and gets rid of stale air, and it also has a heat exchanger that can recover heat from the outgoing air and preheat incoming air. To use an HRV properly, you should be running it 24 hours a day. However, is this efficient? Could we put it on a timer to run in 30-minute increments, in other words, run for 30 minutes, shut off for

Filtered air is healthier air. Clean air results in better indoor air quality. When you're planning a renovation, ask your contractor about air filters and proper ventilaion for your home.

Mike's TIP

Go with the flow: The importance of ventilation

Ventilation matters because it's going to keep your walls and floors and fixtures from getting moldy. It matters because it's going to keep the shingles on your roof from deteriorating more quickly than they should. And it matters because ventilation goes hand in hand with insulation to reduce your energy consumption and therefore your heating and cooling costs.

So what's involved in good ventilation?

First and foremost, make sure you have high-quality fans in your kitchen and bathroom and that they are properly vented to the outside—and use them a lot. (I'll say more about this in later chapters about kitchen and bathroom renovations.)

Second, make sure your roof and attic are properly vented—according to code, at a minimum. Unfortunately, some roofers neglect to do even this. Get that air moving through your attic, and have attic fans installed if necessary.

Third, open your windows now and then, especially on the second or third floor of your home. You need to pull in that fresh air from the outside.

30 minutes? That would be wise, because you're going to save energy but still have continuous fresh air.

A poorly installed forced air system can be noisy, and it can also waste a lot of heat. One major source of heat loss is the ductwork. If the ceiling is open in your basement, you can inspect your ductwork; during a renovation, while walls are open in other parts of the house, is another good time to check this. What are we looking for? Holes from nails and screws—heat can escape there. Also, have the joints and seams in the ducts been sealed with mastic and seams taped? Where you have the chance, I would recommend that you tape all your joints, using metal tape, not conventional so-called duct tape. If there are holes in the ducts, tape them up, too. One thing I like about old forced air systems is that the ducts are of thicker-gauge metal—when you're renovating, it's always best to keep the older ductwork if you can.

You can cut other heat loss with insulation. If ducts run up an exterior wall, they should be insulated. Though you'd be exceeding the minimum code requirements, I highly recommend that you always insulate your ductwork, in both interior and exterior walls. Duct insulation is essentially conventional fiberglass insulation backed with paper. It wraps right around the duct. Insulating ensures that less warm air is lost, and because the duct itself is kept warm, it doesn't need to heat up before it starts pumping warm air throughout your home. Building code states that ductwork on interior walls doesn't need to be insulated because if it does leak, it will leak into your home. I disagree with this reasoning, since if you allow even a small percentage of air loss, the specified air flows have been decreased and the proper amount of warm air may not reach every room.

Whether you upgrade or insulate your ductwork,

Whether you upgrade or insulate your ductwork, keep it clean

always keep it clean. I was removing an old system recently. As I pulled down the cold air return, I nearly fell over. It was disgusting, full of dust and probably dust mites—the worst thing you have ever seen. Imagine the lungs of someone who smoked two packs of cigarettes every day. And that's how you want to think of your air return—as the lungs of your home.

Today, there are high-velocity heating and cooling systems that I really like. High-velocity systems force the air through the ducts at a high speed, actually creating currents of warm air in the rooms of your home. One of the great aspects of high-velocity systems is that the ducts they use are very small—just 2 inches in diameter. Contractors can snake them through all sorts of places where they can't run standard-size ductwork. These high-velocity systems work well, and they don't have the fan you find in forced air systems, which makes them very quiet. But again, if you run this system on an outside wall, it must be insulated. We must always think both about getting the warmth where we want it and about energy efficiency. If your furnace is running continuously, you are wasting fuel and dollars.

Whether you are buying a home or planning substantial changes, you need to keep the furnace in mind. Here are the questions to think about: How old is the furnace? How much longer will it be good? You'll want to get an expert to check if the furnace is running at its full strength, because over the years—just like the engine of a car or our own bodies—a furnace will start to lose its oomph. As well, lots of people don't understand that their furnace was designed to heat the home as it was built. So even if you were to gut your house, put in new ducts,

Insulating all the heating ducts in your house (not just the ones on exterior walls) cuts heat loss and makes sure that the right air flows all through your house.

Electric heating can be installed under tile floors

A viable way to provide warm-floor heating in smaller spaces, such as bathrooms or mudrooms, is to use an electrical radiant heat system that has wires embedded in a plastic mat. The mat is adhered to the floor over a layer of thinset mortar (top photo). The mat is then rolled out over the mortar (middle photo). After the mat is installed, another layer of mortar provides adhesion for the finish flooring, often tile.

and insulate the hell out of it, you might still have heating problems—if your furnace is no longer the right size for your house. Too small for the house, too large, or too old—whatever the case may be, a renovation may be the time to think about a new furnace, particularly one of the high-efficiency models that are out there now. If nothing else, an HVAC expert can rebalance your furnace to make sure that it is running efficiently and getting heat (or cold air) to all parts of the house evenly. This is actually a fairly simple procedure. The HVAC expert can determine if some vents should be closed off to redistribute the flow of air in your home and can blow fog through the system to check for leakage if your ducts are visible.

RADIANT HEAT

I think the best heating in the world is radiant heat. It's the most even, comfortable form of heat because it works by actually heating the floors, walls, and objects in a room, rather than by just blowing warm air over them. Radiant heating systems can also be very efficient.

Traditionally, a radiant heat furnace has a boiler attached that heats water; this is connected to pipes that carry hot water or steam throughout the house. Most people with older homes heated by those old hot water radiators want to keep them. Of course, there are pros and cons to everything we use. The cons are that radiant heat is a dry heat and the heat could be uneven in your home. To balance it, you have to have some sort of stand-alone humidifier in your home if you live in a colder climate. Another problem is floor space. Those old cast-iron radiators do take up a lot of room. It's possible in older homes to convert to smaller baseboard-style radiators. And I'll tell you something I don't like about radiators: When you have pipes running

Hot water in pipes under the floor provides very comfortable heat

The PEX Warmrite radiant heating system. Warm water goes through a manifold (bottom) to flexible Ipex pipes under your floor. It can even be used outside to melt snow on your driveway (top).

throughout a house, inside walls and under floors, you always have to think about possible water damage if a pipe leaks or bursts. Even these problems, though, are not that hard to fix.

What is the best radiant heating out there? If you are planning a major renovation and are willing to pay the considerable up-front costs, I'd suggest changing your whole home to in-floor radiant heat using durable plastic cross-linked polyethylene (PEX) tubing throughout. The tubes are usually embedded in concrete. This system can be used under any type of flooring, including certain types of hardwood, though ceramic or even concrete floors make the most efficient use of radiant heat. This eliminates the need for radiators on the floor. And ductwork—which can blow dust, dirt, and mites through your home, a particular problem for those with allergies—would be a thing of the past.

I can think of only two drawbacks to radiant heat. First, when you want to change the temperature in a room, it takes longer to make that happen than it would with a forced air system. Second, without ductwork, you no longer have a built-in way to get central air conditioning throughout your home.

ELECTRIC HEAT

Electric heat is my worst-case heating scenario. Running an electric furnace costs way too much money and it's not efficient. I wouldn't install it, and if I had it I would think about replacing it with a different type of system. The only type of electric heating I would use is in-floor electric radiant heat. This is probably the most energy-efficient electric heating system there is. Like a PEX system I mentioned above, it is an in-floor

If you switch from an oil furnace, the law requires that you get rid of the old oil tank. At one job (above), we had the nasty surprise of a buried oil tank in the backyard. Not a good idea.

heating system. It's essentially a custom pad with coils running through it—imagine something like an electric blanket. It can go under tile, stone, or even laminate or engineered wood. It keeps your feet warm, and if your feet are warm, you're warm. If you were renovating just one room, especially a kitchen or bathroom, it might be the cheapest way of getting a better heating system.

OIL HEAT

Whether your home is heated with forced air or radiant heat, the most common fuel today is natural gas. Time was that it was oil. But oil has fallen out of favor in recent years, in part because of the cost of oil compared to natural gas (though relative prices are always subject to change), and in part because of environmental concerns about contamination: A quarter of a gallon of oil can contaminate 1,000 gallons of water. But furnace oil (which is almost exactly the same as diesel fuel) may in fact become popular again, especially if the new biofuels are as good as promised. Made from soybeans or corn, biofuels are mixed with furnace oil to create a fuel that doesn't rely as heavily on fossil sources.

But the contamination risks remain, especially with old oil tanks. Even if your home is now heated by a fuel other than oil, you still need to ask yourself the following: Was your house ever heated by oil? Is there still an oil tank somewhere on the property? Sometimes the tank can be buried outside. Is it empty? At one house we renovated in Toronto, the tank had been capped off but the oil left in it. Water got in and rusted a hole in the steel tank. This can be a potentially catastrophic event. We are talking about removing tainted soil from your yard, from your neighbor's yard if it gets there, from under the street—even from a

Mike's TIP

Geothermal heating

Geothermal heating may sound like the world's most innovative heating system, but it's actually quite old, dating right back to the Romans.

A closed-loop geothermal system is based on the simple fact that if you go underground at least 6 feet, the earth's temperature is always the same year-round, between 60°F and 68°F (15°C to 20°C). Here's how it works. Pipes are connected to your home's radiant heating system (or a heat pump) and buried 6 feet underground. As a glycol fluid (essentially antifreeze) is pumped through the pipes, the fluid is warmed or cooled to the temperature of the earth. In the winter, the heat from the earth is extracted to heat your home and in the summer it can be reversed to absorb the heat from your house. If you're still cold or hot inside your house, you can also use an auxiliary heat source to warm or cool the fluid slightly—and it will only have to be slightly.

Typically the underground pipes in a geothermal system are run horizontally 6 to 8 feet underground, but you can go vertical if you don't have the land space. Geothermal systems are highly efficient and can save energy. It's definitely a technology to consider.

mile away if it leaches into an underground stream. We are talking tens of thousands of dollars. So be aware if you're buying a house that has an old oil tank sitting in the basement or buried in the yard, and if you are getting rid of an old oil furnace, that you must remove the oil tank in a very short time frame.

SOLAR HEATING

Solar heating uses systems that won't be found in the basement. In fact, they don't fit our traditional definitions of how to heat a home: The furnace isn't inside the house because the "furnace" is the sun itself, and the heat is collected outside the house, usually on the roof or on a free-standing panel.

Solar heat has come a long way. When it first came out, those big panels really did take up a lot of roof space, and they were an ugly addition to your home. Now there are many different types of solar heating systems, and they've really increased the energy they can store from the sun. Solar could be a good option for a renovation where, say, you're doing only one room. You could use a solar energy system to run electric in-floor heating. Is it the best system? Well, operating it is always very cost-efficient, but it's the setup costs you have to look at. Then there is the question of how much sunlight your area gets, and its intensity. For those who are very concerned about leaving a "light footprint," though, the environmental points of solar will weigh heavily—after all, there may not be a more environmentally friendly form of heating than this one.

With the progress that's being made in solar technology, I can definitely see solar furnaces becoming the norm in new-home building. The possibilities for savings are endless. You can easily search the Web to find out more and maybe make contact with one of the specialists in this fast-growing field. Of course, you'll want to do as much background checking on these contractors as you would for any other—and maybe even more, because this area is changing and growing so quickly.

The Electrical System

Whatever else around your home you think you can do, electricity is one area for the experts only. Electrical codes are complex and stringent, and it takes years to become a licensed electrician. Fool with the plumbing or the drywall, and you might embarrass yourself; mess with the wiring, and you could end up dead.

That said, let's take a look at what kind of electrical system is running your house (or a house you may be looking at) right now. Somewhere in the basement—almost certainly in the utility room, if there is one—you will find a black or grey metal box called a service panel. (In some warmer climates, you may find the electrical panels installed on the house exterior.) This features a heavy cable run in from the outside, to the frames or "buses" inside the service panel that the circuit breakers connect to. Circuit breakers are switches, often with labels indicating what part of the house they are for. Each circuit is designed for a certain load of amperes ("amps" for short), a measure of the electrical current the wiring in that circuit can withstand. All of the lights and devices that you run off your circuits are rated for wattage, which is the amount of electricity that they consume. You see this on light bulbs most obviously, but most home appliances—from toasters to TV sets to computers—also give their wattage. By the way, some devices, such as newer televisions, video equipment and computers, draw a small amount of power even when off: The "off" setting is really a form of standby for a society that has a hard time waiting. Multiplying the number of amperes in a circuit by the voltage tells you the total number of watts that particular circuit can safely stand. A 20-amp circuit, for example, can power 2,400 watts' worth of lights and other equipment. The safe capacity, however, would be much lower—80% of the total.

▶ ▶ ▶ **HOW MUCH IS ENOUGH?** When you're evaluating the electrical service, you need to think about your electrical needs based on the way you live. Most often, people talk about the electrical service size of a house by citing the number of amps it can handle—you'll hear about 60-amp, 100-amp, or 200-amp service. Every service has to have a main disconnect, either a main switch or a main breaker. Every breaker has its ampere capacity (ampacity) marked on it, almost always on the end of the breaker lever or handle. A main switch will often have fuses, which are marked with their ampacity. The meter outside your house may tell you, but that doesn't mean it's correct. You should talk to a licensed electrician, who can easily tell you the service size in your house, which is the maximum amount of power available to be used.

How many amps is enough? In an older home you're likely going to see a 60-amp service. For most of the 20th century, 60 amps was enough because we didn't have as many electrical devices to operate as we do today. A good guideline to remember is that you can't exceed twelve devices per 15-amp circuit. (A device can be anything from a switch receptacle to a light.) That should tell you whether 60 amps will be enough. If you upgrade to a 200-amp service, which is today's norm in the U.S., that is a lot of power, but it's also becoming the norm for modern families, so you'll definitely want to upgrade if you're

Only a licensed electrician should be working on your service panel

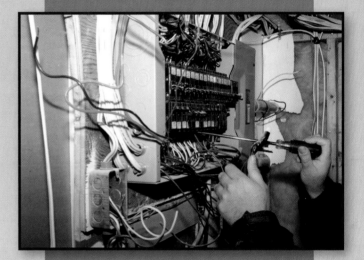

Top: An electrical panel with circuit breakers (the black switches). The bottom photo illustrates why you want only licensed electricians working in your house. By code, wires should be stapled to the studs, and notching studs to feed wires through is not acceptable.

thinking about resale value. With 200-amp service, you can run a washer and dryer, an air conditioner, your forced air heating. At the same time, however, you might want to think about what you can take off your electrical panel to ease up on the load. You might think about taking out your electric hot water heater, for example, and putting in gas. That would clear some space on your electrical panel for other devices.

Any time you want to add more electrical components, you have to look at possibly upgrading to a 200-amp service. The more devices you add, the more power you're going to need. Ultimately, though, the big question isn't whether you have 60, 100, or 200 amps. Safety means working within what you have and determining if it was installed correctly. More on that later.

Most houses now have circuit breakers, but if you have a fuse panel—a real possibility in an old house—don't be afraid of it. Why do we no longer have them? Simply because circuit breakers are much easier. They're designated for specific amperages—15-amp or 20-amp, say—and the moment that amount is exceeded, they'll flip the circuit off. Fuses work in much the same way: They are designed to blow before the wiring in the walls heats up. The problem with fuses in the past was that people had too many appliances and light fixtures and not enough fuses, so they kept blowing fuses. They got tired of that, so what did they do? Instead of putting in a 15-amp fuse, they upped it to a 30-amp fuse. That fuse won't blow, but it also won't stop the wiring and connections from heating up. Instead, the wiring and connections heat up to the point of failing (if you're lucky), or to the point of igniting something. People didn't know how to use fuses properly, but instead of educating them, we changed the building code to get rid of fuse boxes. If you keep your fuse box, educate yourself about the wire size (known as the wire gauge) in each circuit so you can use the right fuse for the job. Or, if you are planning electrical upgrades, bring in an electrician to look at whether it should be replaced.

Now let's look at the different wiring possibilities.

Another nasty electrical surprise. Speaker wire connected to electrical wire and an improvised wire clip of a nail and electrical tape. All electrical connections should be in an accessible junction box.

KNOB AND TUBE

The oldest wiring, which was installed up until about 1945, was called knob

When dealing with wiring in any renovation, always try to think 10 steps ahead

and tube. This featured two separate wires, one black and one white, for each circuit, not the single plastic-enclosed wire carrying the supply, return, and grounding wires that we are used to today. (And in a lot of instances, the wires were not color-coded except at switches and outlets.) "Knob" and "tube" refer to the ceramic knobs (insulators) that the wires were strung on through the house and to the ceramic tubes used to pass the wires through joists and studs without rubbing against the wood. Nowadays, it's a minimum code requirement that if you gut your home and it has knob and tube, you must replace it. Most insurance companies will not take out new-home insurance policies for houses with knob and tube. However, if you are buying a house with knob and tube, an insurance company may arrange a temporary policy that allows you to upgrade within a specified period of time.

In most cases when you're looking at an older home, you'll hear that the knob-and-tube wiring has been changed. But what I often see is that not all of it has been changed, only some of it. Whether it's a cover-up or a financial thing or both, I don't know. Maybe the current owners of the house just don't know because they've never opened the walls. One clue can be if the house has intact plaster walls but there are new electrical switches. What is in there?

The big problem with mixing new wiring with old

wiring is that they were designed for different amperages. If you overload the older circuit, you can have a fire. If you are looking at a house with a mind to buying, you want to make sure you have somebody with you who knows what they're looking for, just to see if it has been changed. How long ago it was changed can make a difference, too. Here's one good way to check: If the previous owners had it changed, ask to see the permit. If they don't have the permit, your local building department should have something on record. Always remember: Permits are like the map to your house.

ALUMINUM

From the mid-1960s until the 1970s, aluminum was used quite extensively for residential wiring. It looked like a cheaper alternative to copper, but like knob and tube it now has a bad reputation. Aluminum wiring itself is not really scary—the problem is how we've made the changes to it over the years. Aluminum wiring requires aluminum-wiring rated receptacles and aluminum-wiring rated switches. Anybody who thinks they can upgrade just by putting in new switches and plugs is sadly mistaken. Aluminum wire also heats up a lot more easily than copper, and it expands and contracts differently. If aluminum wire has been tied into copper using tape or a Marrette (a small connector used for tying wire together), over time

Mike's TIP

GFCI testing

All GFCIs should be tested once a month. To test the receptacle GFCI, first plug a light into the outlet. The light should be on. Press the "test" button.

If the light goes out and the "reset" button pops out, the GFCI is working.

If the "reset" button pops out but the light stays on, it hasn't been wired properly and you should call an electrician.

If the "reset" button does not pop out, the GFCI is defective and should be replaced.

the connection between them will loosen. This is where what electricians call arcs start. The wire comes loose and the electricity literally jumps, or arcs, to the nearest conducting material or between the two wires, creating great heat and potentially starting a fire. To avoid this, with aluminum wiring everything must be rated for use with aluminum wiring—circuit breakers in the panel, receptacles, switches, lighting—it all must be AL-rated. If you have aluminum wiring but don't plan to replace it, it's important that you have a licensed electrician who understands it come in and take a thorough look and fix any inadequate connections to switches, receptacles, or splices. If you're nervous about it, you can always get rid of it. Copper is definitely the easiest, and of all the materials available, it's the best conductor.

WIRING FOR SAFETY AND CONVENIENCE

When you take a look at the wiring in an old house, it's not uncommon to find a spaghetti factory of attachments and new wires. One of the houses we featured in a show was probably the worst electrical nightmare I have ever seen in my life. We found a total of 41 electrical junctions in the basement that had been covered up—which is unsafe, and violates the electrical code. That was just in the basement. As we continued to work through the house, we found more. In those 41 basement junctions, I found every type of wire possible: aluminum, ungrounded wire, even some knob and tube. It had everything—right down to speaker wire being used to carry electricity.

We found that the refrigerator—which, by good practices, should be on its own circuit—was tied into other circuits, all of which were overloaded. I cannot believe that that house did not burn down. To be honest, if you see something like this in a house that you haven't yet bought, you might be a little leery of purchasing that home. At the very least, be aware that you'll have to spend some money to make it right and safe. In cases like these, I highly recommend you bring in a pro to take a look at it and make sure it's functional and safe. And sometimes, there's no way to be sure unless you open up the walls. All the walls. There's a point at which problems in the wiring you can see are indicators of serious problems in the wiring in the walls. Then it's time to completely re-wire the house.

Even if your home's electrical system doesn't require a major overhaul, you might want to carry out some sensible safety modifications. Ground fault circuit interrupters (GFCIs) protect people from severe electric shocks and electrocution. Because you're at a greater risk of getting a shock when you're wet, the National Electrical Code (NEC) requires GFCI protection (either a GFCI receptacle outlet or a circuit with a GFCI breaker) for all receptacle outlets in bathrooms, kitchen counters, garages and unfinished outbuildings, unfinished basements, and outdoor receptacle outlets, among other places.

▶ ▶ ▶ **How does a GFCI work? When you plug something,** like a hair dryer, into an outlet, electricity flows from the shorter slot (hot) to the taller slot (neutral). A ground fault happens when some of the current leaks or escapes to the ground, especially if you are acting as the pathway to the ground. A GFCI monitors the amount of current flowing into hot and returning on the neutral; if there is a difference—even as small as 4 or 5 milliamps, even amounts way too small to activate a fuse or circuit breaker—it cuts the electricity in a fraction of a second.

And for bedrooms, we've now moved to arc-fault circuit interrupters (AFCIs), which are similar to GFCIs but where, if certain kinds of arcing is sensed in the wiring, the power is cut off by the arc-fault breaker in the panel. The bedroom historically was the No. 1 place where fires started, so AFCIs are now the minimum code requirement for each and every receptacle, light fixture, and smoke detector in every bedroom of the house. If the breaker senses anything to do with a short or an arc, it will trip, stopping the flow of electricity and very likely preventing a fire. If your state has adopted the 2011 NEC, know that most other living areas of a house will also require AFCIs.

▶ ▶ ▶ **When dealing with the wiring in any renovation, always try to think 10 steps ahead.** Try to design for what you may want in the future. Regarding outlets, for example—where do you want them? How, generally, do you plan to set up your rooms? If you don't think about it first, most electricians (if they don't really care about what they do) will just run outlets every 10 to 12 feet, because that's the standard practice. But putting them in the right location is a very smart move. Let's look at those bedrooms for a moment: I would try to keep my receptacles away from the bed and near the nightstand. Some electricians will even recommend putting a three-way switch by your bed—how many times have you gotten undressed, tucked yourself into bed, and then realized you left the overhead light on? So now, above the nightstand, you can have a three-way switch to shut off that light. As I said, these are things to think about before, not after, when any further changes will cost you much more time and money.

While thinking ahead, you should do a bit of thinking about all the other wiring you might have in your house. I'm thinking now of speaker wires, phone lines, fiber-optic cables, coaxial cable, you name it. If you are involved in a renovation, you could easily run some 1½" ABS piping right through the house to fish future wires through. How many times do I hear people say, "Oh, I just went through the renovation, but I never thought of speaker wire." So now they've got to run the speaker wire around the room for their surround-sound.

In fact, running some ABS piping is a good idea for all future wiring you might want to do. You can do this on every outside wall of your house. You can do it in every interior wall, from floor to floor. Map it out. Later, if it's there, you can use it.

Plumbing

Somewhere in the basement, you'll find a feed line that comes into the house from the city's water supply, or, if you're in a rural area that isn't connected to a municipal water source, from your own well. This main line will split, with one line heading to your hot water heater, the other providing the cold water. Plumbing essentially breaks down into two elements: the feed lines and the drains, which includes the stack. Let's look at each of them in turn.

If yours is an older home, one that's never been modernized, you're going to find galvanized steel or cast-iron pipes running along under the joists and up the outer wall of the house. They will be held together with fittings and elbows that thread onto the pipes. The great virtue of galvanized piping was its strength—it didn't need to be protected against freezing by an insulated wall. There might have been a couple of times during the winter when the lines would freeze and you would be without water, but the pipes would not break. The great drawback with galvanized—one discovered over time—was that scale (mineral deposits) built up

on the inside when the iron reacted with minerals in the water. That gradually reduced the amount of water that got through.

Copper, which had been used before for plumbing and which came to be considered a better alternative to galvanized, didn't have this drawback. Also, it was much easier to work with: A plumber simply soldered the pieces together, rather than having to create threaded fittings. Copper did have one major disadvantage: It froze faster than galvanized, creating flooding problems. That's why, when it comes to installing new copper feed lines, you want to make sure they aren't run on an outside wall. Sometimes you don't have a choice—there's just nowhere else for them to go, and in that case they need to be well insulated all the way around to prevent freezing.

It took years to make the change from galvanized to copper (or to one of the other modern alternatives, rigid plastic PVC or ABS piping). Why? Well, the simplest explanation is that you can't teach an old dog new tricks. It takes a long time for the pros to make changes because they're used to doing one thing day in and day out. They have all the tools and they know the techniques.

Today, another wholesale change is going on in plumbing—a switch to PEX, a flexible plastic piping for feed lines. Some brands of this new piping is made of aluminum sandwiched between two layers of heat-resistant polyethylene, which makes it strong, highly resistant to freezing, and easy to work with. Because it's flexible, very few junctions are needed. What's best, all the feed lines connect to a manifold. For each water use in your home (hot and cold water for the tub, hot and cold water for the kitchen sink, and so on), there is a spot on the manifold. You can shut them off independently of one another, and the water is fed to each fixture separately

Flexible PEX pipe makes plumbing faster and better

Cross-linked polyethylene tubing, known as PEX, is an excellent choice if you have the opportunity to replace the plumbing in your house. Flexible plastic pipes (aluminum sandwiched between polyethylene) are easy to work with, require fewer junctions, and are highly resistant to freezing. Separate lines can run from the manifold (top) to each fixture in the house. Water pressure stays the same everywhere, no matter how many people are using the water at once.

so that you won't suddenly have the water pressure drop in the shower because someone turns on a faucet downstairs.

Another innovation to think about if you are going in for a major overhaul of your plumbing is a tankless or on-demand hot water system. These units heat water only when it is needed. Not only are they energy-efficient, they save space. Conventional water heaters take up a chunk of floor space in your basement. An on-demand hot water unit is wall-mountable and must be vented directly to the outside. We no longer need a chimney for the line to go up because it is directly vented to the outside and pulls in its own fresh air. It is a brilliant system. Although the up-front costs are much higher than if you purchase a conventional water heater, the savings over time are worth it. It's a mistake to buy the cheapest tankless water heater. You should buy a three-stage firing system that allows you to run two showers and a faucet at the same time—one stage on the first faucet, the next stage on the second faucet, and so on. And also keep in mind that you have to run your hot water at 2.5 gallons per minute in order to fire it up. In other words, you can't trickle the faucet—you have to open it.

Somewhere in the basement, you are also going to find what's known as "the stack" (sometimes called the "waste and vent stack," or simply the "vent stack"). Generally a vertical pipe 3 or 4 inches in diameter, the stack takes all the drain water from inside the house—from sinks and bathtubs and toilets—and runs it down through the drainage pipe in the basement that carries it out to the city sewer system (or, in a rural area, to the septic tank). If you look at your house from the outside, you'll notice that the stack goes right up through the roof, too.

PVC pipe (white) should be used for below-grade drainage pipes only.

Vent it right and breathe easier

Every ventilation fan in your home has to be vented outside the building. Some shoddy contractors try to cut corners by exhausting the ventilation fans into an attic or crawl space. Test your bathroom fan by holding a paper tissue up to it while it's running. If the tissue stays in place when you let go, your fan is doing its job.

Because it is open at the top, it allows sewer gas to escape without smelling up the house (that's why it's called a vent stack). It also provides the air that the system needs to drain properly. It is hard, but not impossible, to move the stack, so it is often best to plan any renovations involving bathrooms or kitchens—anything requiring drains— around it. The maximum distance of use is 5 feet from the vertical stack. If you put your toilet or drains farther than 5 feet away from the stack, you'll have to run a separate vent line or air line behind it.

In an older home, if your plumbing has not been touched, you will have lead waste pipes leading from your sinks and toilets to the cast-iron stack. We really don't want lead in our homes, but because these pipes are handling only your waste water—not the water you're going to drink or shower in—it's not a huge worry. In a newer home or one that has been renovated substantially,

your stack will likely be made of ABS plastic.

You can think of the stack as the interior part of your house's drainage system. But it also continues on the outside, as the water is carried into the sewer (or septic tank). In an older house especially, there are a number of possible concerns you might have with drains at this end. The most common problem with drainage pipe comes from deep tree roots that push against, wrap around, and eventually break the pipe. Even without provocation from tree roots, old clay pipe just breaks down over time. To find out if there are drainage problems, here are the questions to ask: Do you normally have any backups? Have there been any floods? Look for signs of backups in the basement. When it comes to drain pipes, the standard rule is ABS for the stack and PVC for the in-ground drainage. They aren't going to corrode, and they're highly resistant to mineral buildup.

Backer board is your best bet for wet areas, such as behind tiles in a shower and tub. Don't settle for green wallboard—long-term, it's not up to the job.

A final word on plumbing. As with electricity, if you're planning a renovation anyway, try to think ahead. For instance, if you are having some plumbing done now but think you might like a bathroom in your basement at some point in the future, why not have the plumber rough in a vent and pipes for a future bathroom? It's easier and cheaper to do it now.

Taking the Inspection Above Ground

Once you've finished with the basement, it's time to move upstairs. The two rooms that have to be checked most carefully, once you've finished with the basement, are the kitchen and the bathroom. (Coincidentally, these three spaces—the kitchen, the bathroom, and the basement—are the three most popular areas for home renovations.)

THE KITCHEN AND BATHROOM

What are we looking for in these two rooms? If you're doing a check on your own home, you'll want to do a couple of things. First off, run some water in the kitchen sink and see how quickly it gurgles down the drain. Then, in the bathroom, flush the toilet. Flushing the toilet is a good way to check drainage within the house. If everything has been run right in the first place and nobody's compromised anything with haphazard renovations,

odds are you're not going to have any problems with the flushing. The water will run right out.

One reason you might have slow-flushing toilets is improper venting. We need air behind the water when we flush the toilet. Let me explain. It's like a plastic pop bottle full of water—turn it directly upside down, and it just dribbles out or comes out in fits and starts; punch a hole in the bottom, and the water races out. So if you flush that toilet and you don't see that cyclone going down the drain, there's probably a venting problem. It could be that there's a very long run of pipe set at a very shallow angle, or it could be that someone's mucked with the stack. A plumber can help you find the problem.

You'll also want to look for signs of mold and rot. Along with the basement, kitchens and bathrooms are the parts of the house that are almost continually wet to some degree, and, with time, water will have worked its way with them. Look under the sink in the kitchen. Do you smell something? Odds are it's mold. Feel and look at the underside of the countertop around the sink, and look for where the water shut-offs are located under the sink. Can you see rot or mold in those areas? Do the same thing in the bathroom, and also check the tiles around the tub—another great place for mold and water damage. Test the exhaust fans in both rooms: They are there to help you control moisture. Turn on the fan and put a piece of paper towel up to it; see if the fan's suction will hold it in place. If it doesn't, it's not doing its job.

Look at the windows, too. Is there condensation? It's easiest to spot condensation when it's cold outside. If you see condensation, that's a sign the house is trapping moisture or has poor air movement. If you plan to renovate either of these rooms, it will give you a great opportunity to deal with your mold and moisture issues.

DRYWALL

I typically call drywall the "cover-up," because that is often what it is used for: to cover a multitude of sins in your home's plumbing, heating, and electrical. Of course, most of us don't want to look at the plumbing, heating, and electrical, so drywall serves an aesthetic purpose, too: It gives us the clean, uncluttered, finished look we want as the starting point for decorating a room. But there's an art and a science to drywall, too, so we need to understand it.

Since the end of World War II, drywall has pretty much been the standard interior wall material. It's made by taking wet gypsum (a soft mineral also known as calcium sulphate) and sandwiching it between two layers of heavy paper. When this dries, you have a rigid board that can be easily trimmed to different sizes by scoring it with a knife and then breaking it, or by cutting it with a saw.

There are different types. There's a more dense drywall in a variety of thicknesses designed for ceilings, thinner types for creating curves, and ⅝", which is fire-rated. Ceiling trusses are often spaced 24 inches apart, and normal drywall isn't strong enough to make those spans; it would sag down between the trusses. Green drywall has been, for years, the No. 1 drywall for use in bathrooms and kitchens—anywhere there is moisture. Unfortunately, it's actually nowhere near waterproof; it's a very light, water-resistant drywall. As soon as it gets really wet, it will mold like crazy. In that it is no different from any other drywall.

For wet areas, underneath tile on floors and walls, a cement board with fiberglass facing is your best bet.

For the rest of the walls in your bathroom, rather than using green drywall, use Georgia-Pacific GP DensArmor Plus drywall. This is truly moisture-proof: It can sit in water and never, ever ruin. Nor does it mold—there's nothing in it that mold feeds off. It's a little bit harder to work with than regular drywall (it's denser), but that's great, because we want it stronger.

Standard drywall comes in 4' x 8' sheets (longer and wider panels are also available), and it is installed by screwing it to the studs with special drywall screws. Then the edges are covered with paper tape and with a finishing compound typically referred to as "mud." After several layers of mud have been applied and allowed to dry thoroughly, you can sand and prime it and have an interior wall ready for painting. Sounds simple, doesn't it? But doing the job poorly will result in a poor finish. Here's what to look for.

For years and years, plasterers have been using premixed compounds. There are a variety of these. Most plasterers prefer one that has less of what they call "fish-eye"—little air bubbles that show up in the plaster as you apply it. But here's the problem with premixed compounds: They are prone to mold. If you put a little bit of water in a bucket of this compound, then put the lid back on and let it sit for a few days, you'll see what I mean. When you open it up, there'll be some mold sitting on top of the compound. The same thing happens in your home: Mold thrives in these compounds.

Premixed compound is also a weak product, which is why you see cracking in the corners or where the walls meet the ceilings, even in brand-new homes. A better product to use is Sheetrock 90, which is mixed on-site. That 90 refers to its drying time, and that is important. Conventional drywall compounds take a long time to dry, creating the right conditions for mold. Mold is not as hungry in general for Sheetrock 90, and because of its fast drying time, there is no time for mold to grow. If you do end up having mold in the future, it is usually a surface mold caused by the humidity in your home. Also, Sheetrock 90 is stronger than mud (the premixed compound). If we were to use it more, I think we'd have a whole lot less cracking. But—and this is where you start to understand how most contractors think—the problem is that you've got to mix it, you've got to clean up your tools after, and it dries out really fast. Contractors prefer the mud that comes premixed in the bucket or in a box because they can just grab it and

throw it on the walls. They want to save time because they want to make money. What they don't realize is that the more they do in haste to finish a job, the worse they'll look down the road when the job starts showing its true colors.

►►► **Another very common problem with drywall installations is popped screws.** You don't usually see popped screws until you roll on paint. As people are rolling the paint on, they tend to push fairly hard, and as they push, the screw pops up if the drywall is not tight against the stud. One quick repair is to plaster it again, but that doesn't really work. You have to add a couple more screws and make sure the drywall sheet is tight to the stud.

Popped screws happen for two reasons. One has to do with a bend in the vertical studs. I'll say more about

A plaster and lath wall. Wooden slats (lath) are nailed horizontally to studs, and then plaster is applied. You can often do a lot with old plaster walls without tearing out all the plaster.

that when we come to framing. The other factor is, of course, the quality of the installation. Drywalling is best done by two people, working as a team. They can get the right pressure on the sheet of drywall to ensure that it goes on tight. But that is not standard practice. There's usually just one guy installing the drywall, working very fast. He has a screw on the drill and just drives it into the drywall, drills in another screw, and so on. Too often today, finishing shows speed, not care. In a new home that's been drywalled, walk right up to the wall and press it with both hands. This will show you if there is any problem with popped screws.

I've called drywall the cover-up, but that's not strictly true. There are things that drywall can teach you, especially about moisture. Check especially around the windows. If it's an older house and the windows are newer, you want to check that they have been installed properly. Look for water signs. Do you see streaks under the windows? Do you see any surface mold? If so, that means water is getting in. Generally, with an older home where nothing has been touched, you're going to be okay: You can make sure that renovations, maybe including new windows, are done right.

PLASTER

Like the inner core of drywall, plaster is essentially gypsum, a soft mineral. It traditionally came in the form of a fine powder that was mixed with water and some fibrous compounds; in homes built prior to the 1940s, you'll probably find horsehair. This was then applied over wooden lath—small slats of wood nailed horizontally to the wall studs. Installing the plaster required great skill. The temptation nowadays is to tear out plaster walls simply because they've deteriorated or somebody wants

to do a major renovation, but you can still do a lot with old plaster walls without necessarily tearing out all the plaster.

What I like about plaster is that, at its best, it's very solid. This is true whether it's plaster on lath or what came a little bit later, plaster over drywall. (This was generally a coat of between a quarter and half an inch of plaster, depending on the levelness of the drywall.) A good contractor should be able to make the repairs to plaster.

Here's what I do. I chip out all the loose and deteriorated plaster. Then I prime the area with a high-quality primer so that the new plaster will have something to stick to and I let it dry at least 24 hours. I make up a mixture of DuRock, a very hard product that will match the hardness and density of the existing plaster. I mix it by hand and put on one coat, making sure that it doesn't extend beyond the surface of the wall. (If it does, you'll have to chisel it down later.) Then, for a second coat, I use a sandable Sheetrock 90. For a third and final coat, I use some sort of drywall compound, which I then sand. If the home is well maintained and the plaster isn't exposed to too much moisture (especially flooding), plaster will last forever.

In the case of both drywall and plaster work, the finishing work on a renovation can sometimes tell us about the skill of the people who did the work. What do I look for? I check out their plastering techniques. Is that drywall perfectly uniform-looking? How did they install the doors—are the doors true (not so much level as true, so that when a door closes there's a nice uniform ⅛" on all sides)? Look at where they've put the receptacles and the switches. Look at the trim along the base of the floor. Where you have a 90-degree angle, is the cut they made a nice clean 45 degrees?

Every carpenter should take the time to check studs for crowns (the natural bow in wood). The crowns must all face in the same direction or you will end up with a wavy wall and screws popping out of your drywall.

Did they use what I call "lipstick and mascara"? In other words, did they use latex caulking on all their seams to cover up cracks and gaps? Guys who care don't want to see cracks, and they'll go that extra length and apply latex caulking. If the finishing is bad, it's only reasonable to worry about what's behind it.

Behind the Walls

Normally, we don't have a chance to look behind our walls unless we are in the middle of a renovation. And as long as everything is working, we don't need to. But if we really want to understand our homes, and if we want to be able to talk to any contractor who may come into our home to make changes, then it is a good idea to know what is in there behind the drywall or plaster.

THE BASIC STRUCTURE

Unless you own one of those older solid brick homes I talked about earlier, or stone or even log homes that are still scattered about the country, your house is probably going to be built of stud walls. Stud walls are constructed of vertical pieces of wood called studs, held together with top and bottom plates. These were historically 2 x 4s—that means 2 inches by 4 inches, although modern 2 x 4s are actually only 1 inches by 3 inches. In recent years, however, there has been a move to use 2 x 6s for stud walls, because they're deeper and allow for more insulation in the walls. Studs are typically spaced 16 inches apart, measured from the center of one stud to the center of the next. Building on 16" centers, as it is called, matches the sizing of materials like plywood and drywall sheets, which are 48" by 96" (or 4' x 8'). Where plans call for a door or window, studs must be cut short and then doubled up with another stud called a jack stud and with a horizontal piece or pieces called a header.

In the past 30 years or so, some carpenters have built stud walls using a measuring tape and a nail gun, but they no longer use a level or square to tell them if their stud wall is perfectly upright or if all the pieces are attached at perfect right angles. Instead, they trust that the foundation is level and square, and figure that by using the foundation as a guide, they should be fine. So they take the measuring tape and mark the wall height on the stud. Every stud is cut to that height and nailed together with the top and bottom plates, and the resulting wall is then stood up in place. Then they move on. Many carpenters today also no longer pick up the 2 x 4s they are using for studs and look down them to find the crown. This is the natural bow in the wood, a visible curve. It is crucial to have your crowns all one way. If your crowns face in alternating directions (in, then out; out, then in), you will end up with a wavy wall that will get worse over time. But I can tell you, most of the guys out there do not look for the crowns—not even in the floor joists, which are required by code to have the crowns facing up. This approach can create problems: You may have screws constantly popping out of the drywall. If you are having work done, it is worth asking about this. Will the carpenters measure and use a level? And, in particular, will they check for the crowns? This is one problem you want to avoid.

Have I ever found a home that has been truly level and truly square? No. Walk into the kitchen of a new home and take a look at the countertops. You'll see how

Above: All the structural parts of your house have to be positioned properly to carry the load of your house. If you are considering removing a wall, you should consult a structural engineer to make sure you're not taking out a load-bearing wall.

Always remember: In a renovation, anything is possible

the contractor has either cut into the drywall to make them fit or faked it with a backsplash because the walls aren't square. When the cabinets go up, they finish it off with a trim on top that will give the illusion that everything has been done right. But walls out of square and floors that aren't level can be much harder to work with when it's time to renovate. Try to lay tiles properly, for example, in a room that isn't square; it's very difficult, and many more tiles will need to be cut than if the room had been square. Whether it's your time or a contractor's time, somebody will spend a lot of time adjusting those tiles for that out-of-square room.

▶ ▶ ▶ **The single most important thing about a house's studded structure, though, is point loads.** That is, the weight of the whole house has to be carried properly and continuously right down to the foundation. This doesn't mean long, continuous pieces of wood, though—it means that the studs, joists, and all the other structural parts of the house have to be grouped and positioned properly.

People sometimes don't think about that when they look at interior walls, but they should. If you take down a structured wall (also called a load-bearing wall), you compromise your home. A great example is if you take down a wall and, because you don't know about loads, you just put up a beam above where the wall used to be. The ends of the beam attach to the interior walls, all right, but if these interior walls aren't structural, you have all this weight just resting on the subfloor. This will create such a big repair job that you'll probably have to move out until it's fixed.

It's really simple to spot problems with structure when the walls have been opened up. But even when they haven't been, you're going to see clues. How many homes have I walked into where people have taken out walls, thinking they had proper structural supports in place, and I could see that the ceiling was literally bowed or bent? Sloping floors can be a sign of a structural problem or an indication of age. Look for cracks in the plaster or in the drywall above doorways, too. That's another indication that something is wrong with the structure.

If there's a wall that you think you'd like to move, how can you tell if it's load-bearing? First, find out which way the floor joists go (look at the joists from the basement, or open up a cold air return to take a look). They probably run from side to side across the width of the house. And odds are that your center wall will run at right angles to the floor joists—and that center wall will be your structured or load-bearing wall. But it isn't always that easy. In some cases, there are load-bearing walls that run the other way, depending on how the floor joists run on the second floor.

But always remember: In a renovation, anything is possible. You can take out a structural wall—if you bring in professionals. That will mean putting up a steel I-beam or manufactured wood beam (there are lots of choices) and then making sure that the load is carried down to the foundation. A structural engineer should be consulted.

DON'T COVER UP

When you are doing a renovation, the temptation will always be to leave the walls there. Or, if they are in rough shape, to simply cover them over. Let me say this right now: Never cover up.

We should see the renovation as an opportunity to see behind the walls. Let me give you an example. On a recent job we were doing, we had a wall that appeared to be fine. I generally like to take the opportunity to open up a bit of a wall to see what's behind it. We did—and we found a huge nest of carpenter ants. There were thousands of ants with wings, getting ready to head off and form new colonies— the colony had been there for years. Ants, termites, other creatures, not to mention old wiring and plumbing and moisture zones—these are all good reasons to pull it down and do it again or at least investigate.

INSULATION

Insulation helps keep our house warm in the winter and cool in the summer. It slows the movement of heat between the exterior wall and the interior of the house. So, of course, the quantity and quality of insulation in your home (or in a home you're thinking of buying) could have a huge impact on your heating and cooling bills. In a newer home or in one that has been significantly renovated, what you will find behind the walls might typically be first a

6-mil vapor barrier, designed to stop air movement, most commonly backed with pink or yellow rectangles (batts) of fiberglass insulation stuffed in between wooden 2 x 4 or 2 x 6 studs.

Let's say your house is quite old, in the 80-year-old range. The outside walls are double brick, and on the inside there is strapping on the brick to hold the lath, the thin wooden strips that provide a hold for the plaster. That means that what we have on the inside is probably plaster and lath, or maybe old drywall. So, if you gut it and you plan to insulate, you're going to need to take down the plaster and lath and stud it. A slightly newer home, maybe one in the 50-year-old range, will have exterior studded walls. This will make insulating much easier.

To me, the best insulation that you can put in a home is BASF's Walltite Eco—the purple spray foam that does not require a vapor barrier. If you're not going to gut the walls or don't want to spend the money on Walltite, use Roxul Plus. These are green batts that provide a fire retardant as well as soundproofing, and they carry the same R-value as any comparable thickness of fiberglass insulation. Like other fiberglass insulation batts, Roxul Plus needs a vapor barrier to stop air movement.

VOICES FROM THE ATTIC

If there is one part of the house that truly captures what we mean when we say "out of sight, out of mind," it's the area under the roof—the attic. And once again, it comes back to our old friends moisture and ventilation. Everybody thinks that because you don't want rainwater to get to it, the attic should be totally closed off. That's not quite true. You want to keep rainwater out, not air.

To go back to a concept I brought up earlier—about warm zones and cold zones in your house—you need

Comparing types of
INSULATION

Type (and most common brand name)	R-value per inch of thickness	General uses	Vapor barrier required?	Good to know	Recommended by Mike?
Fiberglass blankets and batts	3.33	Attics, walls	Yes, with all seams taped well	If compressed, R-value is diminished	No
Mineral wool batts	2.30 to 3.87	Attics, walls	Yes, with all seams taped well	Excellent fire resistance	Yes
Extruded polystyrene (rigid) foam insulation	5	Below-grade walls and floors; foundation walls	No	Also creates a thermal break	Yes
Polyurethane spray foam	6	Almost any application	No	Also creates a thermal break	Yes

Mineral wool batts

Rigid extruded polystyrene

to know that your attic is a cold zone. The insulation in an attic is there to insulate the area below it—the warm zone of the house itself. Cold zones must be ventilated, because otherwise moisture builds up in them. Close off your attic and don't let it breathe, and you will soon see frost buildup in the winter on the inside of your sheeting; this is especially true in the northern United States and Canada. Eventually—and it won't take long—there will be so much mold up there that wood will start to rot. And this isn't just a cold-climate problem. Building codes in the southern United States also require that attics be ventilated, to deal with the problems of high temperatures in attics during the extremely hot summer months.

Older houses generally have louvered vents on their gables. The soffits (the underside of an overhang of the eaves of a roof) are made of solid wood in old houses. To improve the airflow through the attic, builders would put vents in the gables. In a house like that, as long as the roof has been properly maintained, there will never be an issue with the attic. I've walked into attics of 110-year-old houses that were great. The soffits might be solid wood, but wood breathes, and with the vents in the end gables, the air can move through. I've also walked into brand-new homes and right away noticed frost on the underside of the sheeting in the attic. Why? Because the space wasn't breathing properly. That frost is nothing more than frozen water vapor that couldn't get out. Those attics will be a source of problems.

So how do you get the attic ventilation right? Roof vents are a start. But get decent ones, please. Look for a vent that the critters can't chew through, that the birds can't make a nest in, that won't blow off, break,

Mike's TIP

What is R-value?

The R-value of any material—usually insulation—measures how well that material resists the movement of heat if the temperature on one side of it is higher than on the other side.

Basically, the higher the R-value, the better the material insulates. You can also add the R-values of several materials that are layered in a wall. You just have to multiply the R-value per inch of thickness for each material by the number of inches of that material in the wall, and add up the totals.

As helpful an indicator as R-value is, it doesn't tell you everything. For one thing, R-value performance tests assume no air movement. That means you can build a wall with a high R-value, but if you don't then protect the wall properly against drafts, you've wasted your money.

Moisture also has an impact on R-value: Even a small amount of dampness can dramatically reduce the insulating ability of many materials. This is because many types of insulation use the air trapped within them as part of the insulation. Moisture can make the insulating material compress and lose that insulating air. Even a small amount of moisture can make insulation only one-quarter as effective as it's rated.

Roof Ventilation

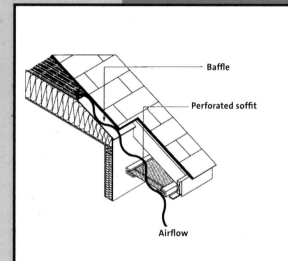

Baffle

Perforated soffit

Airflow

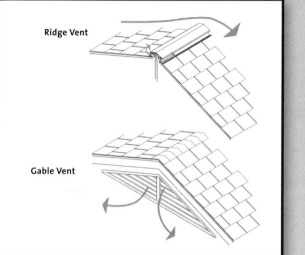

Ridge Vent

Gable Vent

Top left: Soffit vents allow cool air to be drawn into the attic where the air gets moist and warm, and then escapes through the roof vents. With soffit vents you don't need a fan to keep the air flowing, but it's important to ensure that you use a baffle between the insulation and the roof so the air can flow.

Top right: In addition to common roof vents, a ridge vent at the peak of your roof and a gable vent on the sides are great ways to keep your attic well-ventilated.

Bottom: Installing a soffit. Soffits should never be nailed on top of existing soffits—a shortcut that some contractors will take.

freeze, or crack—it's worth the extra money.

In modern construction, you'll see perforated soffits in certain zones that will allow the rafters to breathe. As attic air is warmed, it rises and goes out the roof vents. Cooler air pulled in through the soffit vents warms up in the attic, picks up moisture, and rises out through the roof vents. It's a process that naturally occurs without fans.

So, if this is the way it should be done, why would we have problems? Because so few builders are getting it right. You can see it. The soffit is perforated, but it's been closed off by the insulation. And without fresh air flowing up through the soffits, the roof vents can't do their job.

Renovations on an old house can also mess up the ventilation. A lot of old houses have had brand-new fascia, soffits, gutters, and downspouts installed. I would say that in 90% of those cases, the contractor just covered the old wood soffits with new materials. Why? Because it's more work to pull the wood down and take it to the dump. Anyway, it gives them something to nail the new stuff to, which means they don't have to put up as many nailing edges for their soffits. But the problem is that, in almost every case, they fail to drill holes through the old wood to allow ventilation. Sure, from the ground it looks good—the new soffit material is perforated—but underneath that soffit is solid wood.

You need to inspect your attic. Go up and look around with a good flashlight. Check your ventilation. Make sure you can see an area in the soffit that allows air in every four bays. Don't be surprised—or upset—to see daylight. Daylight is a good thing, because it means air can get in from outside to provide proper ventilation. But watch out for daylight in the wrong place—coming through one of the main faces of the roof, for instance—anywhere that

it could let in water as well as light. Also, look for signs of water penetration, anywhere it might have leaked before; water usually leaves pretty visible stains and streaks on wood. You especially want to take a really good look around chimneys, which are the No. 1 spot for water to get in. And check the insulation between the ceiling joists. Is it nice and deep? Uniform? If you can't get to the attic because it's been closed off by a renovation, that's an issue too: Attic access is required by code.

▶ ▶ ▶ **One final note on attics.** I often see homeowners look at their attics and say, "We can make another room, or maybe even two up there. Even if it's small, let's do it. After all, it'll be cheap, right?" First, understand this: The structure of most homes was never designed to support a room in the attic. It isn't just a question of installing a floor over the floor joists and building a couple of walls. Your ceiling supports are not the same as floor joists. If the trusses are made out of 2 x 4s, how can you make a floor out of that? You can't.

In order to do it properly, you need to cut into the roof and beef up the floor joists so that they carry the weight load to the outside walls. Once that is done, you can create a livable space.

We've now gone through the house from bottom to top. Next, we have to step outside.

CHAPTER FOUR
Outside Your House 101

If you're planning changes to your house, you want to make sure that nothing is going to wreck your investment

You've no doubt heard the term "curb appeal." It refers to the idea that when you're selling your house you should make sure that it looks great from the outside, from the street. But curb appeal is also important while you're living there. Having a home that looks great just feels good. Having a home that looks great and also functions well is even better. And, if you're planning changes to the inside of your house, you'll want to make sure that nothing is going to wreck your investment of time and money. For this, we need the outside to be right. What does that mean?

Above all, it means keeping out water and moisture. Let's continue with our home inspecting, starting at ground level and going up to the top of the house, just as we did on the inside, to see how the elements can damage a house and what we can do to prevent that from happening. > > >

Foundation

When we looked at the basement, our number one concern was water leaking into the house. The best place to stop this is on the outside. The more you protect the outside of the foundation, the better off you'll be and the more money you'll save in the future.

Let's talk about standard practices that affect your foundation. When your home's foundation was built, the builders (hopefully) laid perforated or weeping tile along its base and covered it with gravel to help water flow.

The idea is to carry rainwater and melting snow away from the house, after it percolates down through the soil. Calling it perforated pipe is a little bit misleading. When builders first started using drainage tile around houses (as early as the 19th century), they laid clay pipe right around the house, with the pieces placed in such a way that there were small gaps between each section. The water entered the tile system through the cracks and then the pipe carried it away. Today we use corrugated plastic with slits in it, which is a little more durable. The pipe connects to the city storm drains. (In the suburbs or rural areas, it may be collected into a sump well and then pumped out to ditches.) But one major problem with perforated pipe, especially in older homes, is that the ground above it can compact over time. If the water can't even reach down to the pipe, you can't rely on it to take the water away. Water may then work its way

This photo shows perforated pipe being installed. Nowadays, perforated pipe is a flexible plastic tube with slits on top. Water from the surrounding soil enters the pipe through the slits and then moves through the tube into the city's storm drains. Also note the waffle-like plastic covering the foundation wall—it's protecting the foundation from moisture.

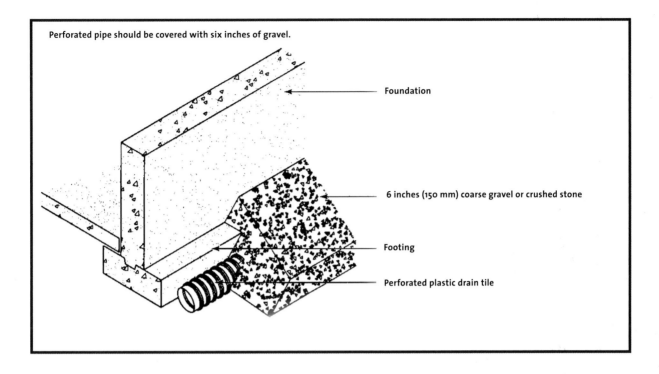

Perforated pipe should be covered with six inches of gravel.

Foundation

6 inches (150 mm) coarse gravel or crushed stone

Footing

Perforated plastic drain tile

into the foundation if the outside of the foundation was not sealed completely. When the water freezes in wintertime, it can push against the outside of the foundation—an especially bad situation for a concrete-block foundation.

►►► **If water is coming into your basement** or you're seeing other signs of moisture, it's reasonable to suspect problems with the drainage pipe. A major excavation to replace the pipe or to coat the foundation with a flexible waterproof barrier (as I mentioned earlier), or even both, is the most thorough plan of action. But there just might not be the room to do a major dig, especially if your home is in an older, built-up part of a town or city. If that's the case, there is still lots that can be done.

For one, grading is essential. You must have a minimum 5-degree slope away from your home, on

all sides, so that water doesn't pool around your foundation. What is a 5-degree slope? If you measure 6 feet away from the foundation, the ground should be 3 inches lower. It's not a good idea to have your downspouts connected into your perforated pipe, either. Have them drain far away from the house. Even where you know the foundation has been made watertight, you want to get that water away from the house.

If you have lots of established trees around your house, see how far out each tree's crown (limbs and branches) spreads. Is the crown brushing your house or near it? The tree's root system covers an area twice that diameter, so it's quite possible that tree roots might be compromising your drains. If you have water coming through your foundation walls or you have a problem with floods, you might want to call in experts to scope your drains. They can put a camera

You may think that "airtight" and "breathable" don't belong in the same sentence

through your basement drains and through your perforated pipe and show you what's in there. If they find weeds or roots, they can run down what is called a sharktooth saw, which will actually whip through the perforated pipe and drain sections and cut out the roots. The problem is that this is only a temporary fix. You may eventually have to replace the section and remove and kill the roots.

If I were trying to create a perfect drainage system to go with the perfect ICF foundation I described earlier, I would use Miradrain. This is a black waffle material, basically just plastic, that's laid against a waterproofed foundation, but the front face is covered with a fabric mesh that draws any water that hits the top of the material down the mesh to the drainage pipe. You can't get a better system because now you're controlling the water.

In some areas of the United States, the minimum code requirements may require that new houses have a sump pump. This is a small pump located in a hole, or sump, in the basement floor. Any water that enters the basement ultimately finds its way to the lowest spot, the sump. The sump pump is equipped with a flow valve that turns it on when the water in the sump reaches a certain height. To me, making sump pumps a standard fixture is a sign that minimum code

construction allows water to get into your basement by not solving the problem from the outside.

The "Skin"

Now let's look at the outside—the fancy dress, if you will—of the house.

When it comes to the outside of your home, you are going to need two things from your outer walls (aside from a look that you like): that they be airtight, and that they be breathable. You may think that "airtight" and "breathable" don't belong in the same sentence. After all, "airtight" means no air gets through, and therefore it's not breathable, right? But there are ways of getting both. You want your interior walls to be airtight so moisture doesn't travel through the walls. Exterior surfaces, like brick, should be breathable.

When we talk about the exterior of a house, we say it's wood, for instance, or it's brick. Many people think they're talking about the structure. But that isn't so. In newer homes, the supporting structure is the stud walls on the inside, which are covered with wood sheathing, usually oriented strand board (OSB, which is a newer variant of plywood), plywood, planking, or possibly exterior drywall. The brick or siding we see on the outside is just a veneer. But don't let the word "veneer"

Wood framing is fast and preferred by many builders

Almost every new house today is built with a wooden frame. Brick or siding is just the covering for the wooden frame. Floor joists are often made of manufactured wood (left), wooden sheathing is nailed to the vertical studs (above), and roof trusses are often prefabricated and then attached to the frame (top).

fool you into thinking it's not important. These various veneers—including their material properties and how they are installed—are vitally important to your home. Each exterior skin has its pros and cons and its own special problems when it comes to protecting your home from the elements.

BRICK

Brick is not waterproof. Sound strange? But think about it: Bricks are made of clay, and clay absorbs water—slowly, but it's still porous. This is true for both modern and traditional brick homes, although older brick homes, with their double thickness of brick, take a longer time to absorb as much water.

If you take a look at the outside of a modern brick home, you're going to see small vertical gaps in the mortar, usually in between the first floor and the basement and in between the first floor and the second floor. The gaps up high are designed to let air in, while the ones down low are to let water out. You'll see little slits above the windows, too. Those will also be for venting air and shedding water. A rainfall will penetrate most common brick in about two hours. This can lead to a problem: I mentioned in the previous chapter that builders nail sheathing over the stud frame of a house. If water gets in behind the brick, what type of sheathing does it come into contact with, and is there any other moisture barrier over that sheathing? Is it an exterior drywall sheeting that isn't moldproof? Is it OSB sheeting? If you're allowing moisture in behind the brick, you're potentially creating conditions for mold to grow.

Although asphalt felt (tar paper) is still allowed in the code in most places, synthetic house wraps are much better than traditional tar paper at protecting the sheathing. Water won't penetrate them, but they're still breathable, because there are microscopic holes in them. This was a good idea. But now there is another question to ask: Is the house wrap on the outside of your home 100% perfect, with all your joints sealed with a sheathing tape to stop air movement and water penetration? Odds are, no, because very often it's just slapped up and stapled on. I would estimate that three-quarters of all brand-new homes aren't taped on all the laps. If water penetrates them, it gets right down to the sheathing, and mold can grow or penetrate your home. Fixing this probably means taking off the brick in any affected area.

One very important way of protecting the interior of your brick home, whether it is solid or veneer, is to keep an eye on the mortar. Crumbling mortar and loose bricks let in water. There are lots of people out there who can do tuck-pointing, which means adding or replacing mortar where the older stuff has fallen out. This is a job that requires a fair bit of skill and practice; it's not a do-it-yourself job.

SIDING

For centuries, siding was made of wood, either clapboards, shingles, or shakes. In the mid-20th century, steel (or, more commonly, aluminum) began to replace wood, and in recent years vinyl has become the most popular siding material. Aluminum and vinyl siding are fairly easy to install and maintain, but aluminum siding can dent, and steel siding can rust. It is the cheapest form of dressing we can put on a house, and because of this we see all the new-home builders trying to use siding as much as possible.

Siding, if installed correctly, is fairly watertight. But siding can and will leak at inside and outside corners and

Vapor Barrier
BASICS

To protect your house from moisture—which will cause mold and rot if it gets inside your walls—you have to come at the problem from both sides: inside and out.

Building scientists are the guys who study how houses work, and there are lots of different opinions about water infiltration and water vapor management. The climate where your house is located will also affect the best way to manage water and moisture. At its most basic, you need to understand that it's very important to keep exterior water out of the house while controlling the escape of moisture from inside the house.

Let's start by looking at where the moisture comes from. On the outside, it's easy: Snow and rain are the primary suspects. Inside, the moisture threats are not as obvious, but they're definitely there. First of all, you've got to remember that warm air rises, so whether it's the heat from the summer sun or the heat from your furnace in winter, you've got air moving in your house. Warm air also holds more moisture than cold air, so any time that moving warm air touches something relatively cold, there will be condensation—that is, moisture. The biggest inside threat, though, comes from those rooms in your house that generate a lot of moisture—the kitchen and bathrooms.

So how do you keep the moisture out of the walls? From the inside, you want to have a vapor barrier, some-thing that will keep any wetness from coming into contact with the studs and insulation. This is always added on the warm side of the insulation—that is, on the inside, just before the drywall goes up.

Exterior house wrap. It's critical for all seams to be taped.

The most common type of vapor barrier used today is wide 6-mil plastic sheeting stapled to the studs, over the insulation. Where the sheathing over-laps, it should be taped to provide a re-ally tight seal. Without tape, moisture can make its way into those gaps be-tween the sheets or into any little hole that gets punched in the plastic. For the same reason, there should be a re-ally good seal where the vapor barrier meets the floor, and around windows and doors.

That's the most common method, but it's not ideal and it's not what I rec-ommend. The problem is that the plas-tic is flammable, and it's almost never sealed properly—most guys are in too much of a hurry to get to the next job. A better alternative is Comfort Foam, the green spray foam from BASF, which creates a total thermal break between inside and outside temperatures and gives you the ideal combination of vapor barrier and insulation. It's more expensive than plastic sheeting, but it creates perfect seals around windows, doors, electrical outlets, and so on.

Now let's look at moisture from the outside. The outer layer—the "skin"—of your house goes a long way toward keeping the structure dry, whether that skin is made of brick, wood, or siding. But any of those is going to let some moisture in, and so we need an-other layer to keep that moisture from penetrating farther and doing dam-age.

The other layer is a house wrap, or moisture wrap, and you've probably seen it on houses as they're being built. A house wrap sheds moisture from the outside even while it allows moisture vapor to flow through its microscopic pores. The air movement allows mois-ture to move back through to the out-side. If there's one problem with house wraps, it's that they require the same kind of taping and sealing as plastic sheeting vapor barriers—and, again, that almost never happens.

Vapor barriers and house wraps are both extremely important, and they should work together to keep your home dry, breathable, and mold-free. How they are installed makes all the difference. There's a lot of careless in-stallation going on out there—make sure your contractor is one of the guys who does it right.

especially around windows if installed incorrectly. This is fairly easy to fix—corners should be caulked, and window trim may need to be replaced properly.

Generally, siding does not keep out the cold. In recent years, however, new thermal-based forms of siding have come on the market, which feature a rigid foam backing. This will give you some R-value, but not enough in my opinion, and they may not be suitable for every application.

FIBER CEMENT BOARD SIDING

Fiber cement board looks like wood, but it's actually a mixture of concrete, sand, and cellulose fibers. It can be expensive and hard to work with, but it won't rot, crack, or burn, and it does a great job of keeping water away from the inside of your home. You do have to paint or stain it, but it holds paint better than most wood siding, it's well rated for the extremes of a northern climate, and it's designed to last for years to come.

STUCCO

In the western areas of Canada and the United States, stucco has always been popular as an exterior finish for homes. The relatively mild western climate is a good fit for stucco, since there's less freezing and thawing. Traditional stucco—a mixture of Portland cement, sand, lime, and water—is relatively easy to apply and maintain and is fairly durable.

I have seen stucco that has been applied right over wood siding. Wire mesh is stapled to the outside of the house, and then stucco is applied on top of the mesh. This is not the proper way of doing stucco. Stucco is porous: It will grab water and pull it in. Water will get in behind the mesh, then freeze and push the stucco off. The right way is to put up rigid foam and apply stucco on top of the foam. And if you're painting stucco, always use a latex paint, not oil. Stucco must breathe.

If you are ever thinking about buying a stucco home, you really want to look at it the day after a rain, when it starts to dry. If you see heavy wet areas on a stucco wall, that means it's holding the moisture. If it takes a long time for it to dry, this is an issue. Above all, you must find out what's behind the stucco. Is it rigid foam? Is it wood? Knock on it. If it has a good hollow sound, that could be foam or wood. As a rule, the older the home (anything that's in the 20-years-plus category), the less likely it is that stucco has been applied over foam.

Today there are newer and better stuccos on the market, such as Jewel Stone from DuRock, which is applied over rigid foam exterior insulation. What I like about this product is that it bonds to almost any surface, and it really works. It's 100% watertight and fire-rated, and it can be finished in a number of ways. It can be made to look like stone, slate, tile, brick—you name it. Now, it takes a true craftsman to do this, but it's good to know that we have better stuccos on the market that bond better and last longer. Acrylic-based stuccos are available, but some trap moisture and don't stand up as well as cement-based stuccos.

WOOD

In my many years in the business, I've met a lot of people who love wooden homes. So do I. Horizontal cedar siding, for example, is a wonderful natural product that resists insects, moisture, and mold naturally. It smells great, too. A lot of other homes, both traditional and modern, are built using board and batten for their exteriors. This consists of 1 x 10 boards (usually rough pine or cedar) run vertically,

Comparing
SIDINGS

Material	Durability	Maintenance	Cost	Recommended by Mike?
Aluminum siding	Relatively durable, but dents easily and finish will wear off over time	May need washing to remove dirt	Low to moderate	No
Vinyl siding	Relatively durable, but prone to dents, cracks, and mold near ground level	May need washing to remove dirt	Low	In limited applications
Painted wood siding (clapboard)	Will last for many years if properly maintained	Must be scraped, primed, and repainted every 2 to 5 years	Moderate to high	Only where home-owners are aware of higher installation and maintenance costs
Stained wood siding (horizontal or vertical)	Will last for many years if properly maintained	Must be restained every 5 to 15 years	Moderate to high	Only where home-owners are aware of higher installation and maintenance costs
Fiber cement board siding	Extremely durable	Must be repainted or stained as needed	Moderate to high	Only where home-owners are aware of higher installation and maintenance costs

Fiber cement board siding

with a narrow 1" batten placed over the seams between the boards. Of course, to work properly, the battens must be sealed.

The problem with a wooden exterior, no matter how the wood is installed, is that you have to maintain it, and that can be extremely expensive and time-consuming. The best way to keep up cedar siding, or even board and batten (if it's cedar or pine), is to stain it if it's starting to look dull or grey. A good way of finding out if your wood is ready to stain again is to put some water on it. If the water absorbs into the wood, then the wood can absorb stain, too.

INSULATED CONCRETE FORMS (ICF)

How do we stop the water from coming in? If I could pick anything, I'd say, again, insulated concrete forms. ICFs can be used not only for the foundation, but right up to the roofline. It insulates and it provides a barrier to water. It doesn't even need interior framing, since there are plastic edges every 16 inches on the inside for you to screw in drywall. And you don't need to stud walls, which saves wood and is thus good for the environment. On the outside of the ICF, you could use a stucco finish of some sort; Jewel Stone would be the best because it's fire-resistant as well as waterproof and 100% adhesive.

Insulated concrete forms don't have to stop at the foundation; you can take the ICF blocks right up to the roofline. You don't have to use wooden studs, the walls provide good insulation, and it can be easily waterproofed.

Together, ICF and Jewel Stone would create a perfect blanket around your home. With siding, brick, stone, anything else, you may still have issues of water and wind penetration; with ICF, you would have a home that would require very little maintenance in the future and save you money down the road. That's how we have to look at a home. How much is it going to cost me in the next 50 years to live in this house? The more water penetration, the more money it's going to cost.

Windows

Often when people buy an old home or start a renovation, one of the first things they do is enlarge existing windows or add new ones. The advantage of bigger windows and more windows in your home is natural light. The disadvantage is heat loss.

Window technology and manufacturing has made giant strides in the last 20 years, but the fact is that every window leaks heat. And every window has a low R-value—right up to a low-E window, which is an expensive, high-end window with a coating that lets light but less heat pass through the glass. This reduces heat loss, but it also cuts down on the possible benefits of passive solar heat. Because windows tend to lose heat, you need to think about them when you're evaluating what kind and size of furnace you need. In general, the more windows you have, the better a heating system you need. And in the summer, more windows can make a home hotter and more difficult to cool. It's a good idea to look carefully at where you install your windows relative to where the light and wind are around your home.

When it comes to keeping cold air out and moisture in, it is essential that windows be installed properly.

You can check this by putting your hand around the casings of all window trim and feeling for drafts. (Using a feather or a burning incense stick also works well.) If you feel a draft around the window when it is closed, the window was installed incorrectly. Ironically, there is nothing in the building code covering window installation. The code does dictate minimum sizes of windows for each room, based on a formula using the room's floor space, but nothing about how those windows should be put in.

Insulating and getting a good air seal around a window are trickier than you might think. Many contractors and new-home builders will insulate a window by stuffing fiberglass batt insulation around the jamb, casing over the window, and then caulking on the outside. But batt insulation doesn't stop air, it only baffles it. I've seen this. You remove a window that's only 10 to 15 years old, and when you look at the batt you see that it's dirty—that's because air is getting through. I've also seen problems caused by builders installing windows with what they take to be a "perfect fit." If the opening is 32" x 32" and the window is 32" x 32", they jam it in tight. They think it's a perfect fit—no heat loss and no air movement, right? Wrong. Wood framing expands and contracts, and so does the window's own framing, especially when the sun is hitting it or it's cold outside. Fit it too tightly and the window won't open or close properly.

The way to deal with both these problems is to leave a small gap around the window—a minimum quarter inch, say—that will allow for expansion. A bigger space—half an inch—around the window is better, because it lets us get a proper spray-foam bead in there. Unlike batt insulation, spray foam stops air flow. The

A properly installed window won't leak

Your contractor should leave a ¼" gap around between the window frame and the wall framing because the window may expand and contract during seasonal temperature changes. The gap is then filled with low-expansion foam (bottom).

kind I use is low-expansion foam—not high-expansion, which could expand too much and also stop the window from opening and closing. As well as foam, you need to have the vapor barrier on the inside extend far enough that it can be tied with house-wrap tape around the window to stop air movement on the inside. Now the window has room to move, but it's also properly insulated and there are no breaks in the protection wrapping the whole house, if it's taped on the outside. If you are replacing your windows, ask the window people about this. It is worth insisting on.

As well, you should buy high-quality thermal windows—watertight and windproof, with a decent R-value. When it comes to windows, there are just so many ways to go. Is it to be filled with argon gas between the two panels of glass? Do you want triple thermal glass? Do you want a window that tilts out from the bottom so that even if it rains you can leave the window open, or do you want side-sliders? It's really to each his own. Do look for high-quality mechanicals, because this is where windows normally break down. Double-glass thermo is sufficient for most homes, and I prefer vertical sliding windows that tilt in. This way you can clean the inside and the outside and still have a full insect screen. I also prefer vinyl windows over a metal or wood frame, for simple reasons: Vinyl is easier to clean, and it lasts longer than metal, which can get scratched or dented. Wood windows are beautiful, but they require more maintenance. Buy good windows and install them correctly, and you'll be spending your money wisely.

Doors

In a lot of new homes, you'll see exterior doors with no protection. Instead of storm doors, I often see just an exterior door open to direct rain, without a roof over it or a small porch. That's too bad. When our exterior doors were wood, we knew we needed storm doors to keep the rain and snow off so they wouldn't rot. Today, most doors are no longer wood. But no matter what a door is made of, if rain hits it directly, water will penetrate the bottom of that door and enter the interior. So always look for protection around doors. Make sure the door is in an alcove, or that there's some kind of roof over it. Or add a storm door. This is extremely important—you want to keep that rain outside, where it belongs.

In general, when checking doors you should be looking for the same problems you might find with windows. Run your hand around the jamb and feel for drafts. If you are replacing an older door, you should consider a good thermal door made of metal with a polyurethane or hard foam interior. These insulate better than wood.

Up on the Roof

To me, the best roof would be a flat roof. Not a conventional one, but what's known as a green roof. It would be green in more ways than one: It would have grass growing on it that could be cut. It would conserve heat better than any other kind of roof. It would allow us to collect rainwater, and to work with nature instead of fighting against it. I think these roofs are going to come into their own in the next few years. But today, the peaked roof, usually covered with asphalt shingles, is still No. 1. This is just what we are used to.

When it comes to constructing a roof, there are two basic building methods. The historical one was to build rafters, of the same general heft as the house's floor joists. The ends were cut on an angle, with a bird's mouth, a notch where the rafter meets the wall, at one end to butt up against

Old shingles should be removed before new shingles are installed

Even though your local building code may allow a second layer of asphalt shingles to be installed over existing ones, this is never a good idea. When the old shingles are stripped, your contractor will be able to inspect the sheathing and other parts of the roof system and make repairs as necessary. Be sure to use an ice and water shield under the shingles and not asphalt paper.

the other rafter at the other, creating the roof peak. Then in the 1950s, the truss system was developed, featuring prefabricated triangular roof supports. Trusses are definitely better.

On the outside, over the trusses or rafters, most houses have sheathing of some kind; very old homes will still have solid wood planks.

▶ ▶ ▶ **When I build, I like to see everything built above code.** I don't use 24 inches on-center rafters. Make it 16. And, ideally, I would specify plywood for the roof, at least ⅝" plywood, not ½". Make it strong.

What type of shingles should you put on? There are plenty to choose from. Clay tiles are common in the Mediterranean and in the southern United States. Installed correctly, they will last for many years. However, they can make for a heavy weight load on your structure, so you may need to consult an engineer.

Most people have asphalt shingles and generally assume they are the best. But they aren't. They emit a lot of nasty chemicals ("off-gassing" is the fancy phrase), and because they heat up so much, they may actually contribute to global warming. But if you're going to use asphalt shingles anyway, do not, at least, use asphalt paper. Spend the extra money on a product like Grace Ice & Water Shield, which is a rubberized adhesive material put on under the shingles. If you cover your roof with this, you've served two purposes: One, you've protected it against ice dams that can build up in the winter at the edge of your roof, and two, you've created a barrier against water penetration if water manages to get under the shingles. Think of it as like a protective washer around every nail. Is it worth the extra few hundred dollars? Absolutely.

Mike's TIP

What is off-gassing?

Off-gassing happens when chemicals are released into the air by a non-metallic substance such as paint, varnish, or glue. Known as volatile organic compounds (VOCs), the chemicals in off-gases cause a wide range of impacts, ranging from relatively mild—stinging eyes, irritated nasal passages, and nausea—to potentially life-threatening.

Any type of construction activity is almost certainly going to bring off-gassing. Paints, particle board, plastics, caulking compound, construction adhesive, and a lot of other construction products contribute to the problem. The worst of the off-gassing happens while these products are curing, which can take months, but the evaporation that causes off-gassing will never really stop. Studies have found that even in the countryside, the concentration of VOCs inside a house is up to 10 times greater than in outdoor air.

Even after the building is finished, hobby activities involving glue, paints, or even markers will boost the VOCs in the air of your house.

Because of the risks of off-gassing, it's best to use low-VOC products wherever possible—for example, latex paints instead of oil-based ones. But it would be very costly and difficult to remove every possible source of VOCs from your home. That's why adequate ventilation that brings fresh air into the house and exhausts stale air and contaminants is your best defense against off-gassing.

Comparing
ROOFING

Material	Durability	Cost	Good to know	Recommended by Mike?
Asphalt shingle	Medium to high	Low to medium	35-year shingles are thicker and last longer, but their actual lifespan depends on many factors, including the pitch of your roof	Yes, if you buy longer-life shingles
Clay tile	High	High	Roofing tile is much heavier than asphalt shingles. You must confirm that your roof can support the extra load	Yes
Flat roof membrane	Low to medium	Low to medium	Proper installation is critical. Decks should not be placed directly on a flat roof	Yes
Steel	High	Moderate to high	Steel is a fireproof material	Yes

Installing the fascia, the front face of the eaves.

This, of course, assumes that if you need to reshingle, you will remove the old asphalt shingles first. And you should, even if the building code says you can have two layers up there. (It used to be three, but now it's two, so I guess that's progress.) I always recommend stripping the roof. Think about it logically. Do you need another weight load on the roof? What are you covering up? Can you really make those new shingles watertight? And is the guarantee on your new shingles still valid if you put them on over older shingles? Call the manufacturer to find out—odds are, it's not. And remember, please, to keep one of the shingle-bundle wrappers; it has the warranty printed right on it. If the shingles fail, you will need that to show to the manufacturer.

One other point about shingles. You'll see some referred to as being good for 25 years and others for 35 years. But do they really last that long? In my experience, no. And a big part of this has to do with the pitch of your roof. The steeper the pitch, the less direct weathering your shingles will take because they will shed water and ice more easily. If the pitch is shallower, they will be exposed to rain and snow for longer periods of time and they will decay more quickly.

In my opinion, the best cover for a peaked roof is steel. There are a couple of reasons for this. Steel shingles usually carry a 50-year guarantee and, best of all, they're fireproof. (Imagine that a fire breaks out next door, and there's a wind blowing burning embers onto your roof. That's how really big fires spread from house to house. If you have a steel roof, odds are it's not going to burn.) Made of galvanized steel with a ceramic type of coating on top, steel shingles can be manufactured to look like traditional ones. There are also versions available in aluminum. Steel roofs are fairly watertight if they're installed correctly. Is it the best bang for your buck? I think so.

The other material on your roof to check out is the flashing—the thin sheet metal around the chimney, dormers, skylights, and so forth. In the case of the chimney, for example, the flashing rests flush against the chimney and then goes under the shingles. This is prime territory for water to get under the shingles. We want to see that the flashing has been sealed with caulking. It's a good move to check your flashing every year, especially around the chimney. Missing or cracked caulking can let water into your house. If you see any signs whatsoever of moisture, get a roofer in immediately.

By now you'll have realized that the exterior of your house is made up of a series of diverse systems. One concern that is common to them all is keeping water and moisture out. Armed with more information, you're in a better position to make sure that your house is—or can be made—both watertight and breathable. Once those concerns are taken care of, you can begin to think about some of the really fun stuff—like what you want on the inside. Let's move on.

CHAPTER FIVE
Bathrooms

Whatever you do, never skimp on the stuff that's out of sight

The wildest bathroom I ever did cost $52,000. That was nearly 20 years ago. A family had a large bathroom designed for them by an architect. I quickly realized that the architect had miscalculated some things rather badly, and I had to rework them on my own. I loved the challenge. The owners ended up with a bathroom that featured a custom shower stall, a half-moon whirlpool tub, a sauna, a cedar-lined closet for towels and linens, and a separate makeup room. I put in full-length mirrors around the tub, and a 4' x 4' skylight over it, with lighting in the skylight tunnel. It was drop-dead gorgeous. The owner was so excited she was pulling in people off the street, even complete strangers, to have a look at it. > > >

10 things to remember about your
BATHROOM RENOVATION

- Permits: Get them. A typical bathroom renovation could require at least three: electrical, plumbing, and structural.

- Make sure you're there for all building inspections. Usually there are two stages to the inspection: the rough-in and the final. Be at both.

- Don't consider a quick-fix solution for your bathroom renovation. You probably need to gut the bathroom to make sure it's done right.

- Invest in a high-quality ventilation fan and make sure it vents outside. Proper ventilation in a bathroom is the best way to fight moisture and mold.

- For proper drainage, toilets should be no further than 5 feet from the vent stack.

- If you are thinking of moving a tub, make sure the structure underneath it is strong enough in the new location. Likewise, if you're putting in a larger tub (such as a soaker tub), make sure the structure can support the extra load.

- If you are considering stone tiles in your bathroom, think safety. Non-slip tiles and glazes are available.

- Don't use green drywall in the bathroom—even though building code allows it. Use concrete board in the tub and shower area and mold-resistant drywall in the rest of the bathroom.

- Buy good fixtures. Better-quality toilets, tubs, sinks, and taps are worth it, but price isn't always the best indication of quality.

- Plan your lighting and electrical carefully before your renovation. Consider multiple sources of light and ensure that you have ground fault circuit interrupter outlets within 3 feet of a water source.

The bathroom is one of the riskiest rooms in the house for leaks, moisture, poor ventilation, and mold

What You Want, What You Need

Twenty years ago, a $52,000 bathroom was unusual, but now more and more people are creating elaborate bathrooms, places where they can get away from everything and enjoy a few minutes of private luxury. They want to add relaxation features such as soaking tubs and steam showers, as well as beautiful surfaces and finishes that make the bathroom feel like a spa.

Maybe your needs and budget are a little different. Maybe you need to replace a tired-looking bathroom that was last renovated 30 years ago. Maybe you need a bathroom for the kids, a powder room on the main floor, or an upgrade of the basic fixtures in your new home. The specifics for each of these projects will be different, but one rule is common to all of them: Whatever you do, never skimp on the stuff that's out of sight behind the walls.

►►► **The bathroom is one of the riskiest rooms** in the house for leaks, floods, moisture, poor ventilation, and mold. Showers and baths generate a lot of moisture to start with, and inadequate or shoddy plumbing just increases the risk of damage caused by water. Today, you can also add electrical overload to that list of risks, because of new but increasingly common features such as in-floor electric heating. That's why everything behind the walls and under the surfaces has to been done properly, and with the best products—proper insulation, breathable products, watertight systems. We also need better tubs, better faucets, better circuits and outlets—better everything, when it comes down to it.

►►► **What's the best way to approach a bathroom renovation?** The first question to ask is this: Why are you doing this, and what do you hope to accomplish? Be as precise as possible when you answer this question. For instance, "We need a new bathroom" will not help you gain direction for the project. Better to say, "We need a new master bathroom that will give each of us ample room to get ready in the morning, that will have lots of storage space for toiletries and linens, and that will be luxurious enough to relax in at the end of the day." The more carefully you define your goals, the more likely you will be to meet them.

Next, as with all renovation projects, you have to ask yourself the money question: How much, realistically, do you have to spend, and what is that amount, realistically, going to get you? The average price of a standard new bathroom is between $10,000 and $20,000. For that

In most cases, you can't just do a quick fix and leave it at that

amount, you'll get a bathroom that's designed and built with simplicity and that looks good. I suggest being prepared for the $15,000 to $20,000 range, however, because it will be worth your investment. If you decide to use more fixtures, and high-end ones at that, you'll find that the cost will easily exceed $20,000.

Whatever your budget, there are some materials and products that should be seen as necessities rather than as extras, even though they will exceed the minimum code requirements. You should absolutely spend money on a watertight system for the floor and tub area, on proper insulation, on concrete board instead of drywall around your tub and shower and on mold-resistant drywall elsewhere in the bathroom, on individual shut-offs for each plumbing fixture, and on a high-quality ventilation fan. Using better materials doesn't cost much more in labor, and the extra $2,000 or so that you spend will be a wise investment in the long run.

Let's look at the project first as an investment, rather than as a necessity or a luxury. If you are looking ahead to what you will get back when you sell, don't be afraid to put the money into your bathroom. It's one of the top three zones in your home for investment purposes. What you get back will depend on the market you're in and the house's overall value, but new bathrooms tend to recoup about 75% of what is put in. You'll find that other people—

buyers—do like new and exciting things, especially in bathrooms and kitchens, so those are fairly safe places to improve. If you want to have some fun and you've got some money to spend, go ahead and give it everything you want. If you are on a tighter budget and you're renovating because you really have to (there's mold behind the tub, or the counter is rotting away), focus on the fundamentals. In either case, be confident about the investment you're making in your house. And in either case, be realistic about what you need to do, then plan carefully: Without good planning, you can spend a fortune and still not get it right.

Renovation Reality Check

How many times have I walked into people's homes and heard them say, "We need new tiles around it, but we'll keep the tub" I have to laugh, because why would you keep the tub, put up a new wall with new tiles, and then have to take it all down again in a few years when the tub needs to be replaced? It just doesn't make sense. In fact, by far the most common mistake that I see in bathroom renovations is the quick tub, toilet, and sink replacement. What happens is that the homeowner goes to a bathroom place or to a bathroom/kitchen store. There are tons of them, and they are well-known, big-name companies, where the goal is to get you in, sell you a bunch of merchandise, and get you out again fast, before you've had a chance to

Bathroom renovations should include more than just new fixtures

The most common mistake I see in bathroom renovations is to do nothing more than replace the tub, toilet, and sink. Take the time to think about how your bathroom will be used and get the fundamentals right.

When planning a bathroom renovation, don't forget space for doors to open and close.

really think things through. They make it sound as if—and I love this: It's the same as when you're buying a car—you can get a new bathroom from $6,395. Yes, everything is "from," but nothing is ever actually sold at that price. It's always twice the cost of "from."

In most cases, you can't just do a quick fix and leave it at that. It's not worth your money, especially if you get sold on one of these "from" packages. Simply replacing the tub and tile, toilet, sink, and cabinets is not going to solve your problems. If you're going to stay in the house, all you'll have achieved is putting off the work (such as proper plumbing and electrical, getting rid of mold, and proper waterproofing) that is going to have to be done eventually. And later, to do the job right, your contractor is going to have to pull apart that quick fix.

Let me give you an example of what not to do. I had a couple call me one time and say they wanted a new bathroom. I went in and I could tell right away that it had been done before. I took a look at it and decided to do a

complete gut. As I gutted, I discovered this was the third time the bathroom had been renovated. I was the fourth guy in there, and everyone else had covered over what had been there before them: drywall over tile over drywall. It was a complete cover-up, with mold galore. There is no such thing as a quick job.

Another example of a so-called quick job is a tub and shower cover-up kit or "the new shower in a box." They actually put an acrylic cover over your tub and new acrylic walls right over your walls. This is a huge mistake. It's a sure thing that you'll be covering up problems. This product—like a ton of others I could name—is a great money-grabber. People think a quick fix is going to save them money, but it doesn't work that way. You do get back what you give. If, instead of one of these quick fixes, you spend your money wisely and you put the right planning process into it, you'll likely get your investment back.

So do it right the first time. Almost every time,

that means gutting your bathroom. Take it down to the studs so you can do a visual inspection of the structure, plumbing, electrical, and insulation, then bring it up to the way it should be—not just to the minimum code requirements, but better. Is it worth it? Absolutely. Be realistic and plan carefully. You'll be spending your money wisely, and you'll have a bathroom that works right, lasts for years, and maintains its value.

Step One: Planning and Design

Now is the time to educate yourself about how to do a bathroom the right way. Step back and think through your needs, the problems you have with your bathroom right now, and the options you have for solving those problems. It's not a coincidence that designers often use the term "design solutions," because much of design is exactly that: looking carefully at how to solve the problems with how a space works. That's what you're doing right now, at the planning stage.

If lack of space is the problem, ask yourself if you can expand the bathroom by stealing a closet or other space from an adjacent room. If not, can you rearrange the fixtures so the space works better, and maybe upgrade with better storage? Or maybe the problem with the bathroom isn't its size, but the number of people trying to use it at the same time. Who uses the bathroom (mom and dad, the entire family, guests)? Does it function as a purely practical place to take morning showers, or should it be luxurious and relaxing? Will you diaper the baby there, let the kids have bubble baths there, or put your makeup on there before evenings out? If you're asking this bathroom to do too much for too many people, would it

Mike's TIP

When don't you need to gut it?

Well, honestly, almost never. That is, almost every bathroom renovation needs to start with a complete tear-out of the old fixtures, floor, tiles, and drywall. But if your job is one of simple upgrading, gutting may not be necessary. Let's say you hate the cotton–candy pink toilet and sink in your powder room. Or you've moved into a new housing development and the bathroom is adequately built, but you don't like the builder's-grade sink, faucets, cabinet, or toilet. These are situations where only cosmetic changes are needed. Go shopping for fixtures that you like, and have them installed by a qualified plumber. No gutting required. But beware: There are very few cases like this. Gutting is usually your best bet.

make sense (and do you have room) to add a new bathroom in another location?

▶ ▶ ▶ **Remember as you plan that you are almost certainly going to have to gut the whole room.** Look at this as a huge opportunity. Once you accept that everything will have to be opened up, you'll feel a lot of freedom as you think through the best layout for the bathroom. Bathrooms are different from kitchens, where the design is really driven by the work. In a bathroom, there are far fewer of those kinds of practical needs. The ways we use each fixture aren't closely tied together the way the fridge, sink, and stove are when you're cooking. In a standard-size bathroom, of course, there's a limit to how many different places you can put the toilet, sink, and tub. And you'll probably want to keep the toilet close to the plumbing stack, because if you move it too far away, you're going to have concerns about the venting, which will add to the cost and complexity of the work.

You will want to consider, though, adding more fixtures than you had before, especially if you've found a way to get more space in the bathroom. Will you want a separate shower stall, maybe even designed so it doesn't need a curtain or door? More space also gives you more placement options for fixtures. Where privacy isn't an issue, some people put the tub by a window so they can look out at their garden or the sky while they're bathing. Others put the tub in the middle of the room and make it a true centerpiece. You can put the tub and a second sink in a room that's separate from the toilet, or put the toilet in a private little "closet" of its own. You can have two sinks in one bathroom so each partner has his or her own.

Aside from the important practical consideration of venting (and, of course, budget), the sky's the limit when it comes to designing your bathroom. I like to stick with simplicity—but that doesn't mean lack of imagination. For example, most people place the bathtub faucet at the end of the tub. For one episode of the show, I put it on the side wall, then ran the plumbing in the showerhead in the regular location and put a section of glass in that wall so it allowed light to come through—there was no faucet to get in the way.

Taking over another entire room for the bathroom (such as a bedroom that you can afford to give up) gives you enough space to go extravagant and make extreme changes—like the bathroom I described at the beginning of this chapter. One thing to avoid is the opposite: a tight bathroom. Try not to force too much into a small space—you'll make it feel closed off, even claustrophobic. Spend the time on design to gain more openness. It helps to think in terms of cubic footage (the total amount of space in the room), not just square footage (the floor area). For example, you might have seen some of the shows in which we removed bulkheads over the tub. Years ago, the standard was to build in that bulkhead because it was believed to help with ventilation and air movement within the bathroom. The builders would usually run duct lines through it, or a simple air valve that wasn't electrical, to allow air to escape. Instead, we installed high-efficiency exhaust fans, vented to the outside, which allowed us to remove the bulkheads. Once we removed the bulkheads and brought the tile up to the ceiling, the homeowners all responded the same way: "Wow! The bathroom looks bigger!" Sure it does, because we're increasing the cubic footage—space above feels as good as space anywhere else. The more we remove unnecessary visual barriers and add clear glass, the more we create the illusion of a bigger space. Removing walls and adding a glass shower stall can make a bathroom feel much bigger, even though the square footage is the same.

You'll also want to plan the lighting in your bathroom. An overhead light is a necessity, but don't make the mistake of installing just one overhead light. Your face may end up in shadow when you use the mirror, and you'll find the light unflattering and probably inadequate. You'll likely want lights near the mirror—ideally, on either side of the mirror rather than overhead—so you can see properly when shaving or putting on makeup. It's always nice to add lights in the shower and tub area, too. I call it "choice lighting:" The more lights you have, on separate switches, the more choice you have about how to light the room at different times of day and night. You might want a dimmer switch for the times when you're taking a bath.

When you've made some decisions about the basic purpose and layout of the bathroom, you can finally think about how you want it to look. Just as with kitchens, there are lots of

It helps to think in terms of cubic footage, not just square footage

This bathroom has the luxury of spaciousness and lots of natural light. The tub takes center stage.

Add accent tiles You can add nice finishing touches when using glass tiles simply by replacing random tiles with a contrasting color.

books and magazines out there that will give you ideas about style, which will include surfaces and finishes for countertops, cabinetry, and walls. Or go to a specialized bathroom showroom to see the latest in soaking tubs and rainwater shower heads, as well as faucets, sinks, and toilets in every possible style, from vintage to contemporary. Of course, you could end up spending a fortune on handmade tiles from France and amazing fixtures from all over the world, but if you have the budget for it, and you and your contractor are making sure the fundamentals are done right, why not?

Imagination is a powerful thing, and anything you can imagine can be done with a bathroom renovation. The only thing to remember is that it will come with a price tag, so don't lose sight of your budget, and hold back a little for the surprises that will inevitably crop up.

Step Two: Permits for Everything— Including the Bathroom Sink

When you're doing a bathroom renovation, you are probably going to get work done that requires permits. Replacing a sink, tub, or toilet is not a problem. Moving an existing sink, tub, or toilet (or installing new ones) requires a permit. Any time you move or install a plumbing fixture away from the stack, there are code requirements. To extend the length or size of the bathroom, you need a permit. Even if you're just putting in a powder room under the stairs, there is a minimum height requirement for head clearance. Any time you're unsure, call your local municipality and ask: Do I need a building or plumbing permit to do this or that? It's very simple.

Not getting the permits is a big mistake, for a couple of reasons. First, not having permits allows the contractor to hide things. Plumbing and building inspectors are another check on whether the work is done right. Even if you are able to be there babysitting your contractor and crew the whole time, you may not know what they should be doing, so you won't know if they are hiding things. Second, if an inspector discovers that you've been working without a permit, he (or she) will almost certainly issue a stop-work order, which will cost you time and money in delays while you scramble to get the necessary permits in place.

Step Three: Let the Gutting Begin

To get it right, you're going to have to do it from the bottom up. As with other renovation projects, if it's time to do a new bathroom, odds are that it's time to upgrade the plumbing and the electrical, and maybe even the structural support. It comes back to the age of the house and what's been done to it before. If nothing has been done to the bathroom, it's almost certain you're going to find a few problems. Even if the bathroom has been updated, you have no way of knowing if it was done right.

The only way to see the skeleton of the room is to open up the walls, floors, and ceiling. Now you can

A toilet drain ready for installation of a toilet. For proper flushing, your toilet shouldn't be more than 5 feet away from the vent stack.

get answers to the big questions: What shape is the plumbing stack in? How about the wiring? Are the outside walls insulated? Are they framed correctly? What about the floor joists—have they been hacked at in the past to run heating ducts, pipes, and wiring? You and your contractor are probably going to find a lot that has to be fixed or upgraded.

Before your contractor begins the tearout, you'll want to have a clear agreement about when you'll have to give up using the bathroom under renovation, and for how long. Most homes, thankfully, have more than one toilet, but you may not have another full bathroom. Make sure you've planned for this by arranging to take showers at your gym, a family member's house, or a really friendly neighbor's.

As the work begins, it's your contractor's job to tape off the bathroom with plastic sheeting to keep the dust from floating into every crack and crevice of your house. As he's tearing out the bathroom, he should be disposing of the waste immediately. Just as at any other stage of the job, cleanliness counts.

Step Four: Plumbing Basics

If you are changing the layout of your bathroom, your plumber will be moving water supply lines (also known as feed lines) and drain lines, and possibly changing the venting to the stack. By gutting the bathroom, which includes removing the floor all the way to the joists, your contractor will quickly find out what the setup is now. This will give him easy access to everything so he can make changes the right way.

It's probably obvious to you why some water supply lines and drain lines would have to be moved, but you might be confused about the business of venting to the stack. Think back to the earlier chapter when we did an "inspection" of your house. I explained that there has to be air behind the water in your drain lines, or you won't get proper draining or flushing. That air comes through the plumbing stack—the thick pipe that goes up through your roof and is open at the top. As a toilet flushes, the air comes in from the top of the stack while the waste goes down the stack and into the sewer line. That's why toilets are usually located near the stack. As long as the toilet is within five feet of the main stack, it's vented through the stack, and you should have enough air for a good, strong flush. But I've seen too many cases where a toilet was moved to the other side of the room without extending the vent line or adding a separate air line to the stack. They've exceeded that 5-foot distance, and they're having to flush their toilet twice.

This also happens when a powder room is added under the stairs or in another tight spot away from the stack. Odds are, it's not going to be vented properly, if at all. Too many contractors or plumbers will say, "Don't worry, we'll put in a cheater valve, which will open up inside the wall cavity to bring in enough air for the toilet to flush." A cheater valve (also known as an air admittance valve or AAV) is one of those little valves you often see under a sink, and it's allowed there. Many plumbing codes allow the use of an AAV for a toilet, but my experience is that they don't work very well for toilets. It's supposed to allow air into the line when water is draining but to stop water or sewer gas from coming out the other way. However, unless there is a massive air drop, that valve barely opens when it's supposed to. Generally, I do not recommend using a cheater valve anywhere, even where it is allowed by code.

A bathroom under the stairs requires proper venting. Some contractors will put in a cheater valve, but most building codes don't allow their use for toilets. The proper way to vent a toilet is through the roof of the building using a vent stack.

It just isn't good enough.

To move the toilet across the room or install it anywhere away from the stack, you have to install a separate vent line. The plumbing code is very specific about venting angles and runs, which your contractor should be well aware of. He should have gotten a permit for this change, and an inspector will examine the rough plumbing (including drain lines and supply lines) to make sure it's up to code before the contractor carries on with closing in the floor and walls around that plumbing.

▶ ▶ ▶ **If you have an older home,** gutting your bathroom may reveal that you have a cast-iron stack and, possibly, a lead tie-in to your toilet. That's how it was done years ago. Replacing that lead tie-in with ABS could cost you extra, but it's the sort of thing a good contractor will have predicted (because of your home's age), told you about, and accounted for in his quote. Depending on the condition of the cast-iron stack, he may have to replace that as well. Your contractor won't know until he gets in there, but the possibility should not come as a surprise, and again, he should have allowed for it in his quote.

We've looked at venting, which has to do with plumbing drainage. Now let's look at the water-delivery side of your bathroom—the supply lines.

Hot and cold water flow into your bathroom through separate pipes. An important thing to remember is that incoming water (both hot and cold) has pressure behind it, and that brings risks—not just of leaks, but of scalding, when someone is in the shower and a faucet gets opened elsewhere in the house. A pressure-balanced

Rough-in for a shower with PEX pipes. PEX pipes require fewer connections and no soldering.

Adding a whirlpool tub to your bathroom is a plumbing and an electrical job. Be sure that you only work with a licensed subcontractors.

shower faucet (which will cost you more than a standard faucet) minimizes the risk of this, since it compensates for fluctuations in water pressure. But if you are changing all the plumbing in the house, consider PEX plumbing that runs everything through a central manifold. The manifold gives central control of the water supply lines throughout the house, and there isn't the same water-pressure drop when more than one line is open.

Another benefit of the manifold system is its central inventory of all fixtures in the house, which allows easy shut-offs in case of emergency. Because this innovative system dramatically reduces leaks and floods, I think insurance companies should offer discounts to homeowners who install PEX. That may happen in years to come.

Even if you aren't able to change over to PEX, your new plumbing work should anticipate any future emergencies. What would you do if you had water spurting out from a delivery line? The obvious solution, if there's an emergency, is to shut off the main water-supply line (usually located in the basement), but there should also be shut-offs under every sink and on every toilet. Fortunately, building codes now require the installation of shut–off valves for every plumbing fixture. Again, quality counts: Don't buy the compression-fitting shut-offs, even though they're cheaper. Buy a high-quality, single-lever ball valve. They work well, they're tested, and they're proven to last a long time.

Step Five: Get the Electrical Right

The bathroom is a water area. Just think about electricity and water: Mixing them can be very dangerous. You should always use a licensed electrician for anything electrical in the house, but for a bathroom it's essential.

Your licensed electrician will know what's required and what permits are needed, and he'll make sure the work is done safely.

If your home is older, the electrical system is likely going to be older as well. This is something to factor into your budget. The electrician may have to remove old knob-and-tube or aluminum wiring, and will probably have to add proper grounding and new outlets. Bringing your bathroom's electrical up to modern, safe standards can be a big job, especially if the bathroom is quite a distance from the main panel.

Over and above your basic electrical needs, a lot of newer electrical devices (such as whirlpool baths and heating lights) are routinely being added to bathrooms, which has an impact on the whole electrical system as well as on the costs of a bathroom renovation. One of the newest and most popular trends is in-floor heating. Because heat naturally rises, heating the floor can be an efficient way to heat a room. And having warm feet—especially if the floor is of a material that tends to be cold, such as tile—increases your comfort level a lot. Most radiant in-floor systems consist of plastic tubes with hot water running through them, though some (such as Nuheat, a product I strongly recommend) use a wholly electrical system, much like having an electric blanket under your floor. Nuheat is a great product—highly efficient compared to older technology, so that it doesn't use as much electricity. But there are important electrical issues here: That in-floor heating system must be wired directly to the panel. It cannot be tied into an existing electrical circuit. And it must have a watertight floor above it to ensure that the electrical never gets wet. You need a licensed electrician to do this work.

Another way to solve the problem of cold floors is to install a heating light or other overhead heat source. This will cost less to install than in-floor heating, but to warm the floor the heat has to travel down eight feet or more from the ceiling. As well, the heat is fairly focused below the light itself. With in-floor systems, the heat is being applied directly from below and uniformly across the floor.

While at the planning and design stage, you will have decided where you want light fixtures and outlets to be installed. Your electrician will refer to your plans, consult you if necessary (regarding the height of wall fixtures, for instance), and run wiring that will meet your new bathroom's needs. With overhead light and wall light fixtures and a ceiling fan, you'll probably need at least three switches in your bathroom, which should be installed at least 3 feet from any water source. Your electrician should also ensure that GFCI outlets are installed for any receptacle that is within 3 feet of a water source.

Step Six: Ventilation: Remember to Breathe

The right ventilation is essential in the bathroom for your house to breathe. Minimum code states that you need either an exhaust fan or a window in a bathroom. I say have both, if at

An electrical radiant in-floor heating system is a good choice for your bathroom.

Mike's TIP

How long is long enough for your fan?

You might not realize this, but to remove all that moist air you've created while taking your shower, your bathroom fan needs to keep running even after you're done—at least twenty minutes longer, according to some people, but I would recommend thirty. Installing a timer on your fan allows you to do this easily, and will really help control moisture in your bathroom. These small preventive measures can add years to the life of your bathroom.

all possible. (Of course, it's not always possible—some bathrooms have no exterior walls.) You want daylight within the bathroom, and you want proper exhaust, especially if the window is closed during the winter months.

▶ ▶ ▶ **A lot of people do not realize the importance of the exhaust fan.** Most people realize that a fan is needed to remove steam and odors, but the bathroom fan also has to exhaust contaminants in the air that come from the rest of the house. These can include off-gases from building materials, sloughed-off skin, waste from dust mites, mold, and many other types of contaminants.

The minimum code requirement states that a switched, 50 CFM (cubic feet per minute) fan or an 20 CFM always-on fan is acceptable. Well, it's been proven that they all fail. They're just not good enough. They do not grab the air and pull it out. As a matter of fact, they usually just spin the air around.

My favorite bathroom exhaust fans are made by Panasonic. One of their newer models runs 24 hours a day on low, and as soon as you turn the switch on, it increases to high. This is brilliant. On low, it runs so quietly—just slowly moving air—that you don't even hear it. On high, it's still quiet. You will spend around $300 for a Panasonic exhaust fan, but it will be money well spent—especially when you think of the "savings" you'll enjoy from a lousy $35 fan that doesn't work. You can combine good ventilation and overhead heat with Panasonic's WhisperWarm unit. It includes an exhaust fan and a heating element with a fan to direct the heat—and even a night light.

The idea behind all ventilation systems, of course, is air movement. You won't just be removing moisture and

One of the worst mistakes renovators can make is to move the tub but not beef up the structure in the new location

contaminants from your bathroom, you'll be improving the air quality within your entire home. As the fan pulls air out, it allows air to come in. This exchange of air is absolutely necessary for a healthy living environment.

Step Seven: Correcting Structure, Insulation, and Sound

With supply lines and drain pipes running under the floor and through the walls, and with the heavy weight load of a water-filled tub, bathrooms pose serious structural challenges. Let's start with the weight issue.

Lots of people want new, bigger tubs and whirlpool baths. You need to think about what will happen if you replace your old tub with one of these units. Standard design specifications are based on one person in a full tub, not two people. And even if you don't go with a specialized unit (a whirlpool or soaker tub), I advise you to choose a better bathtub—which will mean something heavier and stronger than you'll find at the low end.

The minimum code requirement for your floor joists is **2 x 6s**—which are actually 1½ x 5½s. Is this acceptable? No, it's not. It means your house isn't going to fall in, but that floor's still going to bounce like crazy. And without the right support, a substantially increased weight load in a bathroom will crack your tile, cause drywall cracks, and potentially allow water to penetrate the structure. To go bigger, you'll need a floor system that can carry a heavier load.

How is that done? Well, the flooring surface should have been pulled up as part of the beginning of your bathroom renovation anyway, which will have exposed the joists. The most common route is for your contractor to sister in or laminate in new floor joists. This means attaching new lengths of 2 x 8s alongside the existing joists. Ideally, those new boards will run the full length of the existing joists, but if absolutely necessary, you can use shorter sections; the joints will be weak spots, but the additional strength will be better than nothing. The new joists should be glued and then screwed to the old ones, but if you're adding as many as three extra boards for strength, you'll need to use bolts as well.

Remember, too, that if you are planning to move the tub to a new location in the room, you will also have to look at the structure in that new location. One of the worst mistakes renovators can make is to move the tub but not beef up the structure in the new location. In fact, not only have I seen contractors move the tub and not boost the structure, I have then seen them shift the tub and then

As your bathroom is renovated, you should insist on the best products and techniques to prevent mold

hack through the structure to put in the new plumbing! This is something that is absolutely not allowed: You can't move the structure underneath when you move the tub, so you need to address the structure in the tub's new location. It's imperative to the structural integrity of your bathroom and to everything below it.

While you have the walls open in the bathroom, you should consider another issue that ties into structural concerns: insulation and soundproofing. First, this is the time to upgrade your exterior wall insulation—it will save on heating costs and make your bathroom a more comfortable place to be.

As for sound, I hear complaints about this all the time from customers. People don't like hearing water going down the drain or toilets flushing. A bathroom without soundproofing just won't give you enough privacy. You can soundproof the bathroom, now that you've got the walls open, by using insulation that is specially designed to muffle sound. Think about putting in spun mineral wool which provides sound insulation and fire protection.

Step Eight: Walls and Floors: Breaking the Mold

Mold is a problem in just about every bathroom, probably

in 95% of homes. That's one reason why many insurance policies don't provide coverage for mold damage.

The most common place you'll find mold is behind the tile around your tub or shower. The second most common place is the toilet. People often don't realize that many older toilets were installed using a rubber gasket where the toilet ties into the drain at the floor level (today we use wax gaskets). The rubber gasket absorbs water, as it is designed to do, but this allows moisture to get into the floor or subfloor. And the subfloor in most bathrooms is wood—one of the materials mold grows on. So it's very possible that you'll find mold in the floor around the toilet.

The next most common location is around and under the sink. Here the problem shouldn't be anywhere near as drastic as around the tub or toilet, as long as the fixtures were installed properly, but if you are installing new ones, you will want to make sure it's done right.

As your bathroom is renovated, you should insist on the best products and techniques to prevent mold. Let's start with the walls. As far as I'm concerned, wise homeowners state outright that in their bathroom and kitchen and basement, they want mold-resistant drywall—at a minimum. In these areas, you don't want standard drywall, or even green drywall. It may be water-resistant, but it's not mold-resistant. In fact, it will mold like any other drywall. What you want to use on the walls in your bathroom (except around the tub or shower) is mold-resistant drywall sold by many manufacturers.

In the tub or shower area, where there is going to be tile or stone, even mold-resistant drywall won't be enough. You should be using cement backer board. As the name suggests, this is made from the same materials as the concrete that forms the foundation of your home. This means that it is harder than drywall, which is a fairly soft gypsum-based material. Also, instead of being covered with paper, backer board is formed between sheets of fiberglass fabric. It does not rot. There are a number of different brands of concrete board, all more or less the same, the only difference being that some are denser than others. My preference is Georgia-Pacific DensArmor Plus drywall. Working with concrete board is more challenging—it is harder, and for the seams you should use fiberglass tape—but it's a great backing to any tile, for walls or floors.

On top of the concrete board, before tiling, you need a waterproof system like Kerdi. Kerdi is an orange waterproofing membrane made from polyethylene. We put the Kerdi up with a modified thinset mortar. Thinset mortar is a mixture of cement, very finely graded sand, and additives that allow the cement to properly hydrate. "Modified" means that it has had various polymers added to improve the adhesion. Just think of it as thinset with more glue.

Although we want to use the modified thinset as much as possible, between the Kerdi and the tile there is now an issue. The Kerdi waterproofing product is non-porous. Everything behind it breathes, but it itself

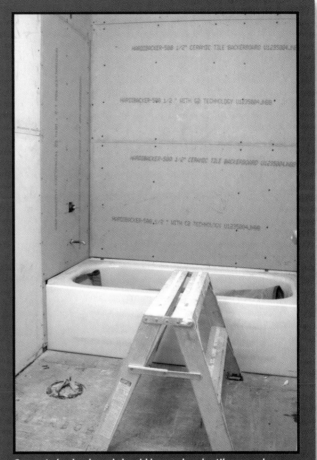

Concrete backer board should be used under tile around bathtubs and showers.

does not: It's watertight. And a tile does not breathe. To sandwich the two together, we can't use modified thinset, because in this situation it would take forever to dry. We need something that's going to dry, so we use the non-modified thinset, which is more like a sandy cement. Then, when it's dry, we apply a standard grout.

There are other little tricks you have to keep in mind as the tub is installed. The tub is going to be slightly shorter than five feet, which is how a tub is designed to go in a five-foot opening. The problem, though, is that at the top of any steel tub there's a lip. That lip is a drip barrier: Any water that splashes against it will flow back into the tub. One mistake contractors frequently make is to bring the cement backer-board for the tiles right down to the tub. In most cases, that lip's not tight to the wall, and to bring the backer-board right down means bringing it in slightly at the bottom, right down to the tub. This makes non-square corners, and because tiles are square, those corners are going to be very noticeable. Tiles show no forgiveness. What your contractor should do is this: bring the concrete board to the top of the lip, fill that 1-inch gap with thinset, and then bring the Kerdi down to the tub. This keeps it true, level, square, and watertight, and makes for an easier and better tile installation.

When it comes to tiling, I see a lot of mistakes in the grouting. It's common for inside corners—where the floor meets the wall or where two corners meet vertically in a shower stall—to crack if they've been filled only with grout. There is movement within our homes through the year, and while we can't prevent that, there are things we can do to keep those corners from cracking under the strain. When those corners are grouted, your contractor should straighten the corner with a scraper to make it 90 degrees, then apply

Preparation of a shower stall is more critical than the finishing. The floor needs to slope properly to the drain (top), there should be a curb to help contain water and the entire shower pan - including the seal around the drain (bottom) - needs to be watertight.

Tile done right should last a lifetime

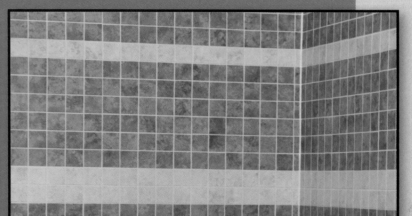

A waterproof membrane, such as Kerdi (top left photo), should always be used before the tile is installed with thinset mortar (middle and bottom left photos). It's also imperative that the tile be grouted—which is the mortar-like material that's pushed into the spaces between the tiles after the thinset has cured. The last important step is to caulk the inside corners and the seam between tub and tile with silicone caulking.

a bead of silicone caulk. If you don't like colored silicone, use clear. Just keep in mind that every inside corner requires a silicone caulking—not latex, but silicone. You want it watertight. Silicone should also be used on the glass around your custom shower to make it waterproof and to adhere the glass to the wall.

In the shower, I like to use Schluter's shower kit—a square, hard foam unit with a central drain opening—to create a foolproof watertight seal. Tile is applied over this. There is no better product. Making sure that tub and shower areas are tiled right is probably the most critical thing you can do to prevent water incursion.

Step Nine: Choosing and Installing the Right Fixtures and Finishes

In a bathroom, you really need to think about the demands that everyday life makes on your fixtures and finishes. Water and rot resistance are really important here, as you can imagine. Almost any bathroom renovation is a big investment, and you'll want to get your money's worth: Not only do you want everything to work, you want it to last for years. Safety is another huge issue. This is a wet area, and you have people climbing in and out of tubs and so on. Finally, you have to be able to clean and disinfect surfaces easily and without the risk of damaging them.

Earlier in this chapter, I recommended spending a bit more for a stronger, heavier bathtub. I recommend the same thing when buying sinks and toilets. It's worth your money in the long run.

A lot of people buy toilets without really knowing what they're getting. They end up with what they think is a great toilet but find out that it doesn't flush very well. Let's remember, years ago the standard was a 5.5 gallon flush, which went to a 3.5-gallon flush, then to a 1.6-gallon flush. The whole theory behind this was to save on water consumption. Now, I am all for water conservation, but the products have to be designed and installed the right way to work with the higher standards, otherwise you actually get more waste, not less. With some 1.6-gallon toilets, you may have to flush two or three times. You already know that this could be caused by improper airflow behind the water, which is related to

When shopping for a faucet, look for a solid brass body and remember that ceramic disk and brass ball valves are better than plastic and steel ones.

With both tile and stone, you need to know how to deal with water absorption

ventilation in the stack. But if that issue has definitely been taken care of, you'll want to look at the design of the toilet itself.

When buying a new toilet, look for a wide throat opening (the throat is the opening at the bottom of the toilet bowl). Make sure it is not the standard 1 ½ inches—you want a much bigger opening. The bigger the opening, the heavier the flush you're going to have.

For taps and faucets, Moen and Delta are equally good. They are both guaranteed for life. I think they are great products. You can go above and beyond, of course, but then you are more into what I call "eye candy." That is, you'll be paying for the design, the looks, and very likely for a more expensive metal such as nickel, brass, or gold, rather than for superior internal workings. And that's fine, as long as you know why you're buying it.

Unfortunately, even the best faucets can cause problems if they're not installed properly. Some plumbers, when they install a faucet set, fail to seal around the base of the faucet. Whenever you splash water, whether brushing your teeth or cleaning the sink and faucet, water gets underneath it. If the water gets through to the cabinet, odds are you will see mold and rot there, sooner or later. Always—whether in the tub or the sink—seal the holes that faucets rest in. Before the escutcheon plates (the finishing plates) go on, the holes should be sealed with clear silicone. Then, after the plates are installed, a bead of clear caulking should go around the edge.

To install a single tap in the shower, the hole should be caulked with clear silicone, with more silicone around the escutcheon plate. You want a thin bead around the top of it

but not the bottom, so that if water gets in there it can still drip out. This also allows it to breathe.

For around tubs and showers, as well as on the floor, I love tile. There are hundreds if not thousands of looks to choose from. Porcelain tile is better than ceramic tile. If ceramic tile chips, you'll see the unfinished ceramic underneath, whereas with porcelain the color is continuous through the tile. It's a little more money, but it's a harder, better tile.

A lot of people want stone for the floors, and it can be a beautiful look in a bathroom. When it comes to concerns or drawbacks, tile and stone have a lot in common. First, both are normally cold to the touch, which you can overcome with in-floor radiant heating, as I talked about in the electrical section. Second, there's safety. I've heard about so many people having accidents in their own

and then seal the whole thing. For one thing, if you grout over porous stone, the grout will penetrate the surface. As well, we want that grout to breathe, because that way any water it comes into contact with can dissipate.

The right way to do it is like this. For waterproofing underneath, make sure there is at least a layer of Ditra (the Schluter underfloor product), with Kerdi-Band (also from Schluter) up against the wall at the edges to make it a watertight floor. Then have your contractor lay out the tiles or stone over thinset. Once the tile or stone is in place, it needs to be left to set for at least 24 hours before grouting. The longer it's left, the better—even up to 48 hours. The thinset should be really dry before the grout goes on.

When the thinset is dry, and before the grout goes on, stone or any other porous tile needs to be sealed with a high-quality sealer, not something cheap: You want it to penetrate the stone, not just sit on top. Two coats of sealer is best—it's enough to protect it, and it will enhance it. There are enhancer-sealers on the market that really bring out the beauty of stone. You can choose a gloss or a matte finish.

bathrooms. People step out of the tub, slip, and break their arm, elbow, leg, hip. You don't want to have a tile or stone that's extremely high-glaze or polished in a wet area. It's just not smart. Today there are great-looking tiles that are non-slip, and stone can also be finished to make it non-slip. Think about going with a non-slip tile in the shower stall as well. And if you do choose a high-glaze tile or a more polished stone, at least have a nice big mat, with a non-skid backing, to step on when getting out of the tub or shower stall.

Another issue with tile and stone is how porous it is: More porous materials absorb more water. You should be able to check the porosity rating of each type of tile you are considering. "Impervious" is the least absorbent classification, followed by "vitreous," "semi-vitreous," and "non-vitreous"—the most porous. Because stone is a natural product, any type of stone has a natural degree of porosity. Limestone, slate, and marble all tend to be extremely porous.

With both tile and stone, you need to know how to deal with water absorption. The first step is to make sure the tile or stone is going to be watertight underneath. Second, with any type of porous material, you need to make sure it gets sealed before it comes in contact with the grout. A lot of mistakes are made by allowing the contractor to lay the tiles, grout,

Choose the right tile, and install it correctly

Choose tiles carefully (top photo) and consider their porosity. Porcelain is less porous than ceramic, and its color is continuous through the tile. If ceramic tile chips, you'll see the unfinished red ceramic underneath. It's important to use a waterproof layer, such as Ditra (bottom photo), under tile. Ditra flexes with minor house movements and helps prevent the tile from cracking.

I always recommend the matte finish because I love the look; a gloss finish will show all the flaws in the stone.

People often ask me about epoxy grout for new tile walls and floors. Epoxy grout isn't necessary if everything is watertight underneath. And I don't like epoxy grout in general, because it doesn't breathe. If you have a watertight membrane like Kerdi behind the tiles, you do not need an epoxy grout. Keep to your standard grout.

People will go to an epoxy grout for a quick fix, and that's a mistake as well. You'll hear a lot of people pushing it as a way to make the tiles watertight. But chances are, if a quick fix is needed, water has already penetrated behind the tiles. Pulling out the old grout and putting in epoxy only traps everything behind it; any problems behind that tile are going to worsen. Don't use epoxy: Just start from the beginning, take it all out, and do it correctly with concrete board and Kerdi on the walls or Ditra on the floor before tiling with a standard grout.

Cork is another good flooring. It's big on the market right now because people want change, they're looking for environmentally responsible products, and cork gives them both. It's naturally resistant to bugs, moisture, and mold. It's a breathable product, and it's a living product—bark from a tree. Is it wise to use it in the bathroom? I'd say it's up to the homeowner. It's a great-looking floor, and it's not cold like ceramic or porcelain or a stone floor.

Finally, a word on cabinets and vanities. When it comes to bathrooms, you should be very cautious about what type of cabinets you install. There are a lot of cheap cabinets out there, some of them well enough designed to look good. But remember: The bathroom is a water area, and anything inside it must be able to withstand exposure to moisture. Cheap pressboard cabinets—especially with exposed edges—can wick up moisture in no time, and then you'll have to replace them. Buy good-quality cabinetry. I'd recommend solid wood with a good finish; it will stand up much better than something made out of particle board. You're going to spend more money to do it right, but in terms of both looks and durability, you'll be glad you did.

There are as many reasons to design and renovate bathrooms as there are individuals and families to use them. Determine your reasons, your needs, your budget, and your style, and you can have the bathroom you've been dreaming of. With the knowledge you have now, you can confidently move ahead with a bathroom renovation that will give back everything you put into it.

Cork flooring is naturally resistant to bugs, moisture, and mold, making it a good choice for your bathroom.

CHAPTER SIX
Kitchens

Don't simply cover things up—get in there and do it right

When it comes to popularity in home renovations, there are three top projects: bathrooms, basements, and—number one—kitchens. Why is the kitchen No. 1? Because not only is it the room you spend the most time in, the place where you cook and often also eat your meals, it's also, for many people, the social center, the gathering place, the modern-day hearth. It's where the family loves to hang out, and it's where guests find themselves drawn, especially with the open, accessible, and attractive way kitchens are being designed today. What used to be a place only for servants is now a showplace, a part of the home that is on display rather than hidden away. And because it's so visible, it has become a favorite place to make a statement about your personal style. ❯ ❯ ❯

10 things to remember about your
KITCHEN RENOVATION

- Permits: Get them. A typical kitchen renovation will require at least two: electrical and plumbing.

- Make sure you're there for all building inspections. Usually there are two stages to the inspection: the rough-in and the final. Be at both.

- Don't consider a quick-fix solution for your kitchen renovation. You probably need to gut the kitchen right down to the framing to make sure it's done right.

- Pick your flooring surface carefully. Wood floors, particularly laminate "click" flooring, are not a good choice in a high-traffic, high-moisture area like the kitchen.

- Make sure the subfloor is right for your flooring material. In particular, don't use a scratch coat (wire mesh and thinset) under a tile floor.

- Seal stone floors before they're grouted. Many contractors wait to seal the tile until after the tile has been grouted, but the grout should be able to breathe.

- When you're shopping for countertops, think about how porous the material is. Granite and other stone surfaces have to be sealed regularly.

- All "custom cabinets" are not custom. Actual custom cabinets are built to order, which takes time. You need to allow six to 12 weeks for custom cabinets. In my opinion it's worth the wait because they're stronger and built to last.

- Plan your lighting carefully and give yourself options. Think about functional lighting under the kitchen cabinets, above the sink, and above the stove.

- Invest in a good ventilation system for your kitchen and ensure that it vents outside your house.

Everyone Wants Wild

Kitchens are getting larger and fancier. Everyone's looking at photos in magazines or watching television shows, and they are seeing wild, dramatic kitchens. Everyone wants one. Fortunately, renovating a kitchen can make great sense financially, because it has a real impact on the value of a home. If you have an amazing kitchen, when it comes time to sell your house you will likely sell quickly, and for a good price. But if you've got an ugly kitchen, your house is probably going to stay on the market for a while and you won't get as much as you'd like, because the new owners will know they'll have to spend a lot to fix up that kitchen.

The nicest kitchen I ever did was for a family that had built their dream home. The kitchen cost about $100,000, with granite countertops, a huge double fridge, wall ovens and a warming oven, a fireplace, and lots of stainless steel. It was a kitchen I liked doing and would have liked to have in my own home. But many people, of course, don't start off with such big ideas. What often gets you thinking about a new kitchen is something far more mundane—something like replacing a countertop that has rotted after years of water pooling around the sink. This is probably the most common motivation for people to say, "Okay, it's time for a new counter. And while we're at it, the cabinets are looking the worse for wear, so let's deal with that, too." Next thing you know, you're in the middle of a major kitchen renovation.

At first, because you may only be aware of problems on the surface, you think you can solve it by calling a kitchen cabinet company. Is it really that simple—you bring them in and they give you a whole new kitchen? Absolutely not. In fact, rather than trying to do a quick facelift on your kitchen, now is the time to slow down and approach your renovation systematically.

What do I mean? Let me give you an example. Let's say that you've bought a home that is somewhere around 40 years old. As far as you know, the kitchen is original to the house. The counter is rotting around the sink, there's mold, and the cabinets are looking pretty tired. Now let's think about what you can't see. If you have to change the cabinets because they're old, you probably need to change other things, too, because they are of the same vintage. The old plumbing is probably just not up to the job anymore, and if you're starting to think about a really fancy upgrade, maybe you'll be adding a sink or two. Then there's the electrical—are the outlets grounded properly, according to today's safety standards rather than those of 40 years ago? Is the wiring aluminum? The house was definitely built in the aluminum era. If so, was it done correctly? How many people have run lines off it over the years, or added circuits? So you may be opening up walls. Time to ask, then, if the insulation in the exterior walls is adequate—if there is any insulation at all. And what about vapor barrier?

If you're looking just at your tired counters and cabinets, these are things you can't possibly know. It's all the things you don't see now that will be the problem. And that's why you don't want a company that just does cabinets. It won't be enough. Just because they know cabinets doesn't mean they understand every aspect of a kitchen renovation. Cabinets are relatively easy. But a kitchen cabinet company does not likely have the talent on staff to explain to you the things you need to know about how to put together a kitchen the right way—I'm talking here about the layout, the plumbing, the electrical, the right surface materials, and, last but not least, how to control and protect against moisture, which is probably the biggest issue in a kitchen. These are the million and one

Good planning and skilled workmanship are obvious in the finished product.

cases people will go to a designer—and stop there. Designers do have a lot to offer. What I love about designers are their incredible imaginations, their knack for putting together colors and materials, for putting the meat on the bones of your dream. But here's the question: Is the designer knowledgeable enough to understand the inner workings of a kitchen (what's behind the walls) and to know how those inner workings need to function together with the fancy bells and whistles in the design they create for you? And if a designer can't do all of that, what route should you take?

All right, let's step back a moment. Any time you want to do anything to your home—I can't emphasize this enough—slow down and educate yourself. Take your time, investigate for yourself, ask questions. You've already got a lot of the answers in your hands, in this book that explains your house from the inside out and from the outside in. You should also check out specialized kitchen-design publications. You'll find a lot of information on efficient kitchen layouts, interesting new ideas and trends, the latest on surface materials, and design ideas for cabinets, counters, built-ins, and even furniture for the hanging-out parts of your kitchen. Reading what's out there and doing a lot of your own brainstorming about what you need will help you answer a lot of questions about how your kitchen should be done.

Where does the designer come in? A really good kitchen designer can make the difference between your ending up with a nice kitchen and the dream kitchen you'd love to have. But, as with any professional you consult, remember that there are good and bad designers. Do your homework before you spend thousands (or even tens of thousands) on their services.

things that make the difference between a kitchen that just looks great and a kitchen that is great, and that will stay that way for years. I've worked on kitchens that looked fabulous, but the cabinets were held on with little finishing nails and the drywall was barely screwed to the studs. You need to go beyond looks.

That's why I'll tell you right now that the older the home, the more you want to look at the possibility that you should be gutting the kitchen. Don't simply cover things up—get in there and do it right. For that, you'll need a multitalented person, or more likely a team of people. And the whole process is probably not going to be cheap. You are looking at $10,000 to $30,000, more if you want to go wild. The older the kitchen, the more updating it will need, and the more expensive it's likely to be.

So who should you turn to? Unfortunately, in many

Step One: Planning and Design: Practical Makes Perfect

Of all the rooms in the house, the kitchen is the one that most needs a practical eye. It's a room that has to be high-functioning in terms of workflow, traffic flow, storage, and even ventilation. So let's start by looking at the kitchen from a practical point of view. Once you do that, you'll discover something really interesting: On the surface, kitchens are all spectacularly different, with all kinds of different looks—there is no such thing as an "average" kitchen—but if you look at kitchens functionally, if you look at things like layout, you discover that they are not so very different.

Why is this? Well, there seem to be some essentials that drive how a kitchen functions. People always seem to want the sink at a window. Why? Because when you do your dishes you want to look outside and dream you're off in some wonderland, or at least somewhere where you're not doing dishes. Or you want to watch your kids in the backyard, or see what your neighbors are up to. Doing the dishes, looking out that window—they just seem to go together. So as much as possible you should try to keep the sink near a window. And even if you don't think it's important for you, remember that when you are selling, this is one thing that people will look for.

Next, you want to keep the sink, the refrigerator, and the range within a triangle, the one we call the "work triangle." With these major pieces of equipment at the three corners of the triangle, you save on the steps you have to take in getting a meal ready, baking something, or cleaning up after a meal. You already know one point of the triangle—it's that sink by the window. It's not hard to place the other two points. In a small kitchen,

Mike's TIP

When do you really need a kitchen designer?

When do you really need a kitchen designer? Many people, given enough time and the right resources, can learn enough to design their own kitchen. But when is this not advisable? When should you turn to a a registered kitchen designer for advice?

- When you don't have the time or inclination to do thorough research. if you're raising children and working full-time, starting a business or a job, or have other urgent demands on your time, you may not have the time to learn about kitchen design.

- If you are not good at visualizing. Some people find it difficult to imagine how a space will look when they only have a drawing as a starting point. If this fits you, you might be better off to spend your time discussing your needs with a good designer who can translate those needs into a workable kitchen design.

- If you're nervous about spending a lot of money on a kitchen renovation without professional advice. You may enjoy looking at books and magazines on kitchen design but not feel confident about your ability to make design decisions. In that case, consult someone who designs kitchens every day and can help you.

Whether you consult a professional designer or not, be sure to consult your contractor about your design. He is vitally important in identifying the structural requirements and limitations of your kitchen (where the plumbing stack is located, for instance), and his experience will have taught him what works.

If you're thinking about resale, remember that most people prefer their kitchen sink by a window.

the triangle will fit right within the room. In a very large kitchen, to keep the distances manageable you might let a peninsula or an island contain one of those major appliances, but still you need that triangle. We worked on one kitchen where the fridge had been put far across the room from the stove and sink, next to the pantry, and in fact it was blocking the pantry door—not a well-considered design.

Start from your work triangle, and the rest won't be hard. For example, the dishwasher normally stays close to the sink, which makes sense: You rinse your dishes, you put them in the dishwasher. You don't walk across the room with water dripping off them to put them in the dishwasher. And then you want the cupboards where you store the dishes to be as close to the dishwasher as possible so you can put them away easily. You need good-sized counters close to the stove, the sink, and refrigerator for food prep, stacking dishes, and loading and unloading groceries. With all the nifty kitchen gadgets today, you also want plenty of outlets. Also, because there is so much traffic through a kitchen, you probably want three-way or four-way switches near all the doors, including any exterior door, so that you never have to walk through a dark room to turn on a light.

Those are some of the basics of designing a well-functioning kitchen. There are dozens of specialized kitchen-design books and magazines, and I encourage you to use them, because they're filled with ideas. Buy or look at as many as possible. But when you look at these

Facing page: Cork flooring can be a good choice for kitchens. Setting cork tiles in patterns will make the most of the available color choices.

kitchens—some of them are really over the top—keep in mind that your kitchen has to work for you. Not just in terms of your budget, which is key, but in terms of the way you use this room. How many people do you cook for, and how often? Is there just one cook, or should your kitchen have room for two people (or even more) to work at the same time? If you bake often, do you want a special section of marble counter for rolling out pastry? Do you want a separate wall oven and stovetop, or a range that combines both? Do you use your microwave for cooking, or just to reheat your coffee and make popcorn? Do you want a desk, a computer, a small family office somewhere in the kitchen? What about a seating area, and maybe even a zero-clearance fireplace or stove for additional heat? What kind of luxury appliances do you have or want—a mixer, an espresso machine, a juicer—and do you want them stored away or always out? Be realistic, get down to the details, and think really carefully about how your kitchen needs to fit with your life. On your own, or in consultation with your contractor and maybe even a designer, you can design the kitchen you've been dreaming of. Having taken the time to consider your needs and wishes carefully, you'll have your design in hand and you can move on to the next step: making sure the necessary work permits are in place.

Step Two: Permits

In the previous chapter on bathroom renovations, I insisted on the importance of getting plumbing permits before the work begins. Just as with bathroom fixtures, you don't need a permit to replace your kitchen sink, but if you move the sink or install a new sink in another location in the kitchen, you will need a permit. It's becoming quite popular to have multiple sinks for different uses in the

kitchen, and even if you don't want this, there's a good chance you'll be moving your sink to a better location, so it's almost a certainty that you'll need a plumbing permit for something. Any time you move or install a plumbing fixture away from the stack, there are code requirements. Adding lighting fixtures or outlets requires an electrical permit. If you are simply changing a light, you won't need a permit.

Your contractor should know the code requirements, and he should take care of obtaining any permits that will be needed for your new kitchen.

Step Three: Go for the Gut

To get your kitchen right, you're going to have to do it from the bottom up. It's probably time to look behind the walls and see what needs upgrading in terms of plumbing, electrical, insulation, and vapor barrier. Besides, if you're implementing a new kitchen layout, you'll likely need plumbing and receptacles in different locations than their current ones.

Make sure that demolition—usually right back to the studs—is allowed for in your contractor's schedule and in his quote. You'll make the plumber's job and the electrician's job far easier, because they won't have to work around existing walls, and because of that you'll probably save money in the long run. You'll also have a finished product that is better by far than a quick fix or facelift could ever be.

Yes, it will be inconvenient to be without a working kitchen while your dream kitchen is under construction. But there are ways to make it manageable, starting with

Don't cover up when you're renovating. Take the opportunity to see what's behind the walls and ceiling.

Mike's TIP

Looking for more space? Facts about bump-outs

One of the most common ways to make a kitchen bigger is by adding a bay window, a bow window, or a bow section. The idea is that you can create a little bit of an extension, get more light for plants or even for seating, just by adding a window that is built out by a foot or two. Is there a problem here? Potentially, yes. For the extra space you gain, it's extremely expensive, and it's possible that it will be done wrong.

With a bay or bow window, you need two things: a contractor who understands the importance of proper insulation and a window installer who understands the special requirements of a window that is more exposed to heat and cold than most other windows. Because a bump-out doesn't have warm space—that is, a basement—under it, your contractor must ensure that it is properly insulated, especially at the bottom. Otherwise you'll be letting cold air right into your kitchen. You can also run into problems with windows that are installed too tightly. Your window installer should be sure to leave room for the window frame to contract and expand with temperature changes, and for a nice heavy bead of foam insulation.

The bump-out is like the whole renovation process in miniature. You want an addition but you can't afford it, so you think maybe you can get some of what you want at a lower price by doing it a different way. But is this the best way? You might just trade off problem for problem: You solve the problem of too little money for a proper addition, but you can end up with a cold kitchen and higher heating bills.

What's the answer? As always, educate yourself and take the time to really think about what you need and what is possible with your budget. Don't get stuck on the idea of a bump-out just because you saw a great picture in a design book. Think it through. Could you use that same money to rearrange the kitchen and get more space instead? If you really need more kitchen space but you can't afford it now, what can you do today that will get you there the right way? Maybe you can make some minor changes that will let you save for another three years to pay for the addition you really want.

A kitchen bump-out, even a small one, is like a whole renovation in miniature. It's one project that you will definitely need a permit for, along with a skilled contractor and a window installer.

a clear agreement with your contractor about exactly when you'll be without the use of your kitchen, and for how long. This is where your hard work in finding the right contractor will pay off, because the best contractors can do an average-sized kitchen, beginning to end, in two weeks.

And just as I recommended in the chapter on bathroom renovations, your kitchen should be taped off as much as possible to keep the dust to a minimum in the rest of your house, and your contractor should dispose immediately of waste from the demolition. That's how good contractors do it right.

Step Four: Plumbing: Water, Water Everywhere

Sinks are a big deal in today's trendiest kitchens. People want a sink under the window for cleanup, a prep sink in the island, and possibly a bar sink in the corner. They may even want a separate faucet near or above the stove to fill pots. And really, it doesn't matter where your sink is now or how many sinks you want in your new design. In a renovation, anything can be moved or placed where you want it. Anything—provided you can afford it, and you get the right permits.

If you have those two concerns taken care of, the next thing is to make sure that each and every one of your fixtures (sinks and faucets) is plumbed properly. What you want to avoid is having those beautiful new sinks, in the exact locations that you've specified, drain slowly. It's a complaint many contractors are familiar with. Why does it happen? Lack of airflow behind the water. Let's go back to the pop bottle example from a previous chapter: Turn the bottle upside down, and the water has a hard time getting out—there's no air. A bit of water gets out, but then air

has to move in through the mouth of the bottle to replace the water that's left. But just punch a hole in the bottom of the bottle, and the water will blast right out. Good plumbing should make water race down the drain—just like that water racing out of the bottle.

People often think that a slow-draining sink is merely an annoyance. But it's more than that. When you rinse the dishes or wash the pots and pans in the sink, you are washing food scraps down the drain. They collect in the trap, which is a curved section of the drainpipe (located just below the plumbing fixture itself) that is always filled with water to prevent sewer gas from coming up into your home. We need the water to rush down the drain and sweep that sludge out to the sewer. There has to be enough air behind the water to make sure that happens. Otherwise, you've created an opportunity for buildups and blockages in the drainpipe. (As an aside, I think it's funny how many people actually want a garbage disposal unit attached to their sink. As far as I'm concerned, garbage disposals were designed for people with too much money. One of the biggest mistakes anyone can make is to fill their drains with garbage—that's just an accident waiting to happen. It should be water, and water only, that goes down the drain.)

► ► ► Sink drainage is really important to think about during a kitchen renovation. Even if your sink drains well right now, that may change if you are planning to move the sink or add another one. In that case, your contractor will have to make sure there is still going to be proper air behind the water. The most important questions to ask are these: How far away from the stack is this fixture going to be? Will it be properly vented? You can answer the first question yourself by locating the stack, which is normally

Make sure that he seals everything that will come into contact with water

very close to the toilets in a house. If it isn't hidden behind the walls of a finished basement, you should be able to see the stack in the basement—it's the largest vertical pipe you'll see, and it normally goes into the floor of the basement and then ties in to the outside sewer system. It also goes straight up through the house and right through the roof. It does that because the stack has two functions: Water goes down it into the sewer system, but the stack is open at the top to let air into the drainage system. That opening is the equivalent of the hole in the bottom of the pop bottle. If the stack were sealed, nothing in your house would drain properly. It provides the air behind or above the water.

So you can see that the farther you move any plumbing fixture away from the stack, the harder it is going to be to get the proper air supply to that fixture. Sure, the building code specifies runs—that is, maximum

distances—for drains that connect a fixture to the stack, and it also regulates things like the slope the line has to be at to ensure that the water runs down into the stack. There is a minimum and maximum slope dictated by the building code. Once you become aware of these issues, you can make sure that your contractor and plumber can handle them.

You not only want to see the drains installed properly, you also want everything to be watertight. As I discussed in the previous chapter on bathrooms, I'm disappointed by the number of contractors who don't make sure that faucets are properly sealed where they make contact with the counter or sink. It's the same with sealing around the edge of the sink—it just doesn't happen. When you use a faucet, you splash water around. Will it get in around the faucets and under

the sink? Yes, it will. It will get into the counter, leaving rot and mold in the countertop and cabinets (plastic laminate counters with a particleboard core are especially vulnerable to this). One thing leads to another, and the renovation cycle will begin again. Remember why you decided to redo the kitchen in the first place? That's right—probably because water getting under the edge of the sink had caused the counter to rot.

What you need to worry about here is technique. By all means, buy those great products you want— that fantastic set of faucets or that really sharp porcelain sink—but also ask your contractor to make sure that he seals everything that will come into contact with water.

There's one more aspect of your kitchen that might require your plumber, if that plumber also happens to be—as many are—a licensed gas-fitter. If you're a serious cook who prefers cooking with natural gas to electric, the gas-fitter will need to move or install the gas lines to the appropriate place in the kitchen. If you plan to have a natural gas fireplace in your kitchen, the line will also have to be installed by a licensed gas-fitter. Your contractor will set this up, but it's good to know what to expect. And crazy as it may sound, in some states, you do not have to be a licensed plumber to install gas piping. Gas is—of course—highly combustible, and should be handled only by a professional.

Step Five: Getting the Electrical Right

When it comes to electricity, the kitchen is probably the most demanding room in your home. And if your home is older, you must expect to do a lot of upgrading in this area. After gutting, you're going to have the walls open, so your electrician will be able to do whatever is needed relatively easily.

So what do you really need? Let's talk basics, what you'll need at the source, from your electrical panel. You'll want to make sure that your electrician allows for, or

In-house sprinklers— help or hazard?

Most house fires today start in the kitchen. And when planning your kitchen it's a good idea—a necessity, really—to think about a fire extinguisher, placed where you can reach it in an emergency. But how about going one step further—with an in-house sprinkler system? I've received many emails and phone calls on this subject. "Mike," the caller will say, "I've heard you talk about making homes waterproof and fireproof and everything else. So I hope you're leaning towards in-house sprinkler systems."

In fact, I'm not. There's no way I want something inside my house that adds another risk of a flood. And remember, in case of a grease fire—which is how many kitchen fires start—high-pressure water is not going to help you. It's probably going to make things worse. Even with fires that start elsewhere in the house, sprinklers won't prevent smoke inhalation. They will cause a lot of water damage, though. Maybe your insurance company likes the sprinkler idea, but they won't like a claim for water damage. It's just trading one problem for another.

A lot of experts have compared residential sprinkler systems to those used in big commercial buildings, and they've found a lot of drawbacks in the residential systems. The water doesn't flow in the sprinkler system for an individual house, so how do you keep that stagnant water from contaminating the drinking water in the house? How do you prevent a plumber who's lazy or doesn't know better from taking a line off the dedicated sprinkler system for something else? How do you prevent a homeowner from puncturing the line when hammering a nail into the wall to hang a picture?

No, a better course of action is to use fire-rated products to make your home fireproof. They're out there—let's find them. Isn't that smarter than bringing more water into the mechanics of your home?

installs, the following: a 15-amp circuit for the lighting; a 20-amp circuit for the refrigerator, and at least two more for the counter–top receptacles (called small appliance circuits); a 20–amp circuit for the range hood; and another one for your small appliances; a 20-amp circuit for the dishwasher; and a 20-amp circuit for a garbage disposal, if you're planning for one. Last, if you plan to have an electric range rather than gas, you will need an additional separate circuit for it, too, one rated for 50 amps and that will deliver 220 volts of power.

Plan where you want outlets to go, too. Think about where you will be using blenders and food processors, about where you want to put a toaster and a coffeemaker, or any other appliances you're thinking of acquiring.

Where the outlets are installed will determine their placement.

And because the walls are stripped away, now is also a good time to upgrade to meet future needs, which may include other kinds of wiring. You may want your electrician to run telephone, Internet, and coaxial cable through the walls if you plan on having a telephone, computer, or television in the kitchen, now or in the future.

Think about your lighting needs, too. Don't just go with one big light in the middle of the room, which a lot of people do. Think about both function and mood. Where will you need the bright lights, the 100- and 200-watt ones? For function, you need stronger lights over the work areas: the stove, the sink, the chopping block. You can put softer lights under the cabinets, install

Great lighting will make a difference in your new kitchen. Think about multiple sources of lighting for both function and mood.

recessed lights in the ceiling, and have everything on separate switches or even dimmers—that will let you use the lights to create an atmosphere.

Many states have energy-efficiency requirements for kitchen and other lighting that require high-efficiency lighting fixtures like fluorescents. Make sure the lighting design—the switching arrangement, and type of light source—meets or exceeds the applicable code.

Remember, when the walls are open, anything is possible. Great lighting can take your kitchen to a new level of impact.

Step Six: Ventilation: Moving the Moisture Out

People often think ventilation in the kitchen is about removing food smells and smoke, and that is certainly part of it. But there's a lot more to it. Kitchens are very damp environments, with dishwashers giving off steam, sinks (maybe lots of them) full of water, and, most of all, moisture from cooking. The statistics are quite surprising: Cooking and normal kitchen chores produce up to five pints of moisture a day. That moisture is released into the air of your house, especially your kitchen. We don't want to put in new drywall and cabinets and then have moisture everywhere.

During a major renovation, you'll likely want to replace your fan, especially if you're thinking of adding a showstopper of a range hood. But if you have a fan that you're thinking of keeping, you should check first to see that it's up to the job. Turn on the fan, put a piece of paper towel up to the fan, and see if it holds it. It probably won't. Investigate what type of louver system you have on the outside of your home for the exhaust itself. Turn it on, go outside, and see if it opens. If you

can, see if the exhaust line was ever insulated. Proper ventilation is another place where you need to put your money. Don't buy a cheap, standard 30-inch fan/hood combination that requires a 4-inch line and costs $50 to $100. Buy the $500 fan. You need really good exhaust to pull the moisture out of your kitchen if you're boiling a pot of lobsters or pasta for 10 people. And the $500 fan will look fantastic.

I'd avoid the systems that promise to recycle the air in your kitchen. You just can't successfully recycle old air. Think of your car for comparison. Imagine sitting inside your car with the windows rolled up. Turn the heating on to internal (recycled) air, an option that some vehicles have. Add some more people. Now we have our exhaled breath and other contaminants, and we're taking the oxygen out of the air as we breathe. All we're doing is moving the air around. This doesn't get rid of moisture. Make sure your fan vents directly to the outside.

Step Seven: The Kitchen Floor—and What's Under It

It won't seem obvious, but the most important thing about your kitchen floor may be what's under it—the subfloor. Is the subfloor as strong as it needs to be for the material you want to put on top of it?

But wait … what do you want to put on top? The obvious (and most exciting) part of flooring selection is how many fantastic-looking materials there are to choose from. And you'll very quickly discover that those materials vary widely in price. So you have three things to juggle: structural needs, looks, and budget. And, because of the different uses a kitchen is put to, you might even want different flooring materials in different parts—something really practical (like tile) in the work area, and something more warm and cozy (like hardwood or cork flooring) in the hanging-out parts.

To guide you through the flooring maze, here are some points to keep in mind on the different materials.

CERAMIC OR PORCELAIN TILES

These are among the most popular kitchen flooring choices, and no wonder: They're durable, attractive, easy to clean, and available in a wide range of colors, patterns, and finishes. Both ceramic and porcelain need a strong and level subfloor to prevent cracks in the grout or loose tiles. (More on that in a minute.) Porcelain is harder than ceramic tile, and even more impervious to moisture, plus it's made with the color embedded throughout, so that chips and cracks are almost invisible. It's also somewhat more expensive than ceramic tile. Tile is durable because it's hard, and that brings some drawbacks: Most glass objects dropped on a tile floor will shatter. A large expanse of tile flooring can also make for a noisy room, because tile doesn't absorb sound. If you're on your feet a lot, tile can be very tiring. And finally, tile can be cold underfoot, though radiant underfloor heating can cure that—for a price. Still, because of their many good points, ceramic and porcelain are my strongest recommendation for kitchen floors.

NATURAL STONE, SLATE, LIMESTONE, OR MARBLE TILES

Natural stone tiles—like most natural materials—are among the most beautiful and longest-wearing of floor materials. They are also expensive, cold, and heavy (requiring strong and level subflooring), and they are difficult to work with. Installing stone or marble is definitely not a job for the do-it-yourselfer. Most natural stone is porous and needs to be sealed every couple of years to prevent staining from everyday use. Setting aside all these disadvantages, however, for the homeowner who loves the mellow, aged, but ageless look of natural stone, there is no substitute.

LINOLEUM

Once a standard feature in the kitchen, linoleum almost disappeared for a while. But in recent years it's made a comeback, in part because it's environmentally friendly. Made of cork powder, linseed oil, rosin, and pigments (for color), linoleum uses only renewable resources. It's durable, waterproof, and relatively scuff-resistant, and it does not burn easily or emit harmful pollutants, as some other manufactured floorings do. Though it's available in a wide range of colors and patterns, it can be difficult to find suppliers and installers of linoleum for residential applications. As well, some people simply don't like the look, which may affect resale potential. I don't recommend either linoleum or vinyl. Both are installed using mastic (a type of glue), which attracts mold. There are some very nice linoleums out there today, but

You get what you pay for with inexpensive peel-and-stick vinyl tiles. They aren't very durable, the vinyl may shrink over time, and the glue can attract mold.

Kitchen floors
AT A GLANCE

Material	Durability	Water resistance	Range of color/patterns	Cost	Environmental concerns	Good to know	Recommended by Mike?
Bamboo	Fairly durable	For limited times	Broad range of stain colors; patterns can be created	Moderate to high	Uses a fast-growing renewable resource	Install much like hardwood	No
Carpet	Depends on grade	No	Broad range of colors only	Low to moderate	Manufacturing process is not environmentally friendly; carpet will off-gas in first months after install	Hard to keep clean in wet areas	No
Ceramic or porcelain tile	Extremely durable	Yes	Almost unlimited	Moderate to high	Uses natural and renewable resources	Subfloor prep is key and grout must be sealed	Yes
Concrete	Extremely durable	Yes (if installed correctly)	Can be stained or painted	Low to moderate	Uses natural materials	May crack	No
Cork	Fairly durable	Low	Broad range of stain colors; patterns can be created	Moderate to high	Uses bark rather than whole trees	Naturally repels water and insects	Yes
Engineered hardwood	Fairly durable	Moderate to high	Broad range of stain colors; patterns can be created	Moderate to high	Uses some natural and renewable resources	Can be dented and and scratched by normal kitchen use	No
Hardwood	Fairly durable	For limited times	Broad range of stain colors; patterns can be created	Moderate to high	Uses natural and renewable resources	Can be dented and and scratched by normal kitchen use	No
Laminates (click flooring)	Somewhat durable	For limited times	Broad	Low to moderate	Manufacturing process is not environmentally friendly	Warranty may be void if used in wet area such as kitchen	No
Linoleum	Fairly durable	Yes	Broad	Moderate	Uses non-toxic renewable resources	Comfortable for long periods of standing	No
Natural stone, slate, limestone, or marble tile	Extremely durable	Yes	Limited to natural colors	Moderate to high	Uses natural but non-renewable resources	Subfloor prep is key and grout must be sealed	Yes
Rubber	Extremely durable	Yes	Limited	Moderate to high	Manufacturing process is not environmentally friendly	Hard to keep clean	No
Vinyl	Depends on grade	Yes	Broad	Low to moderate	Manufacturing process is not environmentally friendly	Mastics are prone to mold	No

Mike's TIP

Wood versus engineered wood

So which one is better: solid wood floors or engineered wood? Actually, that's the wrong question, since there are pros and cons to both of them. Solid wood flooring is exactly what it sounds like: It's milled from a single ¾" thick piece of hardwood. Because it's so thick, it can be sanded and refinished for generations. The big drawback of solid wood is that it expands and contracts a lot as the humidity in your home changes. Contractors usually compensate by leaving an expansion gap between the floor and the wall and covering the gap with molding.

I prefer engineered hardwood. It's made of three to five layers of wood stacked and bonded together with glue under heat and pressure. As a result, it's less likely to be affected by changes in humidity and can be installed at any level of your home—including the basement, if it's been finished right. It can also be sanded and refinished numerous times—probably up to five times over a number of decades—before needing to be replaced.

they cost around $8 per square foot. The average installed price for tile is around $10 per square foot. Why not spend the money and get something nicer and longer lasting?

VINYL

If saving money is your primary objective, vinyl may be your flooring of choice. It's available in many styles, patterns, colors, and grades, depending on how much you're willing to pay. It's also resilient, making it more comfortable to walk or stand on than some other flooring options. Vinyl is usually applied in sheets, and can be tricky to install. Peel-and-stick tiles—the alternative to the sheets—are time-consuming to install. With vinyl, you get what you pay for, but even the top-of-the-line sheet flooring will eventually show signs of wear. Vinyl and linoleum should both be installed over mahogany plywood, because it's the smoothest plywood available. But even when vinyl is installed properly—glued and power-stapled down over mahogany—it's still a subpar choice. That glue is going to attract mold, the vinyl itself can shrink, and there is no remedy for shabby or moldy vinyl flooring except wholesale replacement.

CORK

Cork is one of the newest flooring options. It's made from the bark of cork oak, harvested without felling trees, which makes it a favorite of environmentalists. It absorbs sound and pressure, which makes it comfortable and less tiring to walk on than harder flooring options. And it naturally repels moistures and insects (like cedar does), which makes it a reasonable kitchen choice. It's comparable to hardwood in cost.

Laminate wood floors are made with an inner core of pressed and glued wood material, with a photograph of wood laminated on the surface. They are not recommended for kitchens or other high-moisture areas.

HARDWOOD AND ENGINEERED HARDWOOD

Wood floors, whether solid or made of plies (layers) of wood laminated together, are not considered ideal choices in kitchens. I don't recommend them, because they are susceptible to moisture damage from food and water spills and they can be marked and dented when cans or silverware are dropped on them. True devotees of hardwood may, of course, be willing to accept the risks— and the additional care—in order to have the beauty of hardwood throughout their homes. One advantage of hardwood flooring is its flexibility: The subfloor doesn't need to be as perfectly stable or level as for ceramic tile or other rigid flooring choices.

LAMINATES

Sometimes called "click floors" because they are installed by snapping pieces together over a cushioned pad that rests on the subfloor, laminate floors are made of an inner core of pressed and glued wood material, with a photographic image of wood laminated on the surface. They are extremely impact- and scratch-resistant, but they can be scratched (by a large dog's claws, for instance, or by dragging heavy objects across them). They can be noisy to walk on and, like the hardwood they are designed to imitate, they can be damaged by prolonged exposure to moisture; in fact, their warranties may be void if they are used in high-moisture areas such as kitchens. Laminate flooring has achieved great popularity in recent years because of how easily it can be installed and because of its low cost—about one-third the price of true hardwood. I don't recommend it. Over time, I believe, these products will show their considerable weaknesses.

BAMBOO

Bamboo is becoming a popular alternative to hardwood. Actually a grass rather than a tree, bamboo is a fast-growing, renewable resource. Bamboo floors are installed and maintained in the same manner as hardwood, and like wood floors, they are available in both solid and engineered planks (several plies laminated together). Like wood and its laminate imitators, though, bamboo is prone to moisture damage and may not be an ideal choice for kitchens.

CONCRETE

With the recent influence of the industrial loft aesthetic on home design, concrete flooring has taken hold in the imaginations of some homeowners. It works well with radiant in-floor heating and can be finished with a variety of stains or acid etchings. However, it's hard on the feet and prone to staining. Concrete floors work best when they are an integral part of the foundation—which is not likely to be the case in your kitchen, unless you're planning to cook in the basement, or if your house is slab-on-grade construction. Because of the minimal depth required to pour a solid concrete floor that won't crack or crumble, and because of the joist strength required to support the additional weight, concrete is usually not an option when you're renovating an existing home. Loft buildings, which are made of reinforced concrete rather than wood, are still the most likely places to find concrete floors.

RUBBER

Easy on the feet but hard to keep really clean, rubber flooring has yet to catch on in a big way in homes. Some people like its industrial look and how vibrant its colors are, but there isn't a huge choice in colors and patterns.

CARPET

Wall-to-wall carpeting just doesn't work in kitchens, for the obvious reason that a busy kitchen has lots of water and food being moved around, and the floor needs to be easy to clean. If you choose a hard flooring material without much cushioning (such as tile), you may decide to add some small area rugs, but be careful to use proper skid-resistant underpads to prevent slipping.

So perhaps you know what you like, and what would be the best option in your kitchen. Now let's go back to that issue of the subfloor—what will go directly under the flooring material you've chosen, and what will support the whole thing—because having a strong, unmoving subfloor is particularly important if you want to go with tile of any kind, which is my personal recommendation.

Laying tile properly is the key to its success. If it's laid properly, a tile floor will last for decades without cracked or missing grout or loose tiles. In fact, thanks to a product that is relatively new but that harks back to a centuries-old tradition, your tile floor may even survive the

The ABCs of OSB

OSB stands for oriented strand board—a modern version of plywood that's been growing in popularity since it was first introduced more than 30 years ago. It uses layers of wood flakes, fibers, or strands bonded together under intense heat and pressure. Each layer's fibers run in the opposite direction to the layers above and below, which has a strengthening effect that makes OSB similar to real plywood. There are many manufacturers and grades of OSB, some more expensive than plywood and some less.

A waste of time, materials, and money

I had to rip out what could have been a perfectly good tile floor—if it had been installed right the first time. The first contractor cut corners and laid the tile on a scratch coat of improperly mixed thinset on wire mesh. Bad ideas all around.

occasional dropped item without chipping. Unfortunately, some of today's construction standards and techniques work against a successful tile job, and you need to know why—and how to get a better finished product from your contractor.

▶ ▶ ▶ **To support tile, a floor can't have movement,** and it especially can't have bounce. How much movement or bounce a floor has depends on its subfloor and the joist structure under that. Older homes are normally easier to tile, because they were built with heavier subfloors than today's homes. Go back 60 years or more, and you'll see that those subfloors weren't even plywood (plywood, as we know it, wasn't widely used until after World War II)—they were very heavy planks. And under those planks was a very strong structure. We're talking true 2 x 10 joists, set 16 inches apart.

Today's minimum code requirement is 2 x 6 joists (which are actually 1 ½" x 5 ½", and sometimes as little as 7 ⅛" on a 16" center with ⅝" OSB sheathing over that). Stand in the middle of a room in a modern home and start bouncing up and down, and the floor will move. Now, you won't fall through, but if you put down ceramic or porcelain tile over that subfloor, you will have a problem. Thanks to all that movement, the grout will crack, the adhesive will loosen, and eventually the tiles will come up.

That's bad enough, but 20-plus years ago, the standard method of laying tile was over what we called a scratch coat. This was mesh with a layering of thinset, a mortar designed expressly for tiles. Now, contractors still use thinset today, but here's the thing: On every single bag of thinset it states clearly that if you want to use a scratch coat, you must have a substrate (a fancy word for a subfloor) with a minimum 1 ¼" thickness. That's because it became clear that the scratch coat just wasn't good enough. Yet 80% of all tile installers are still using mesh and thinset on these modern floors that are just too weak. This is an unfortunate demonstration of that old saying, "You can't teach an old dog new tricks." Their attitude is that they know what they're doing, and they don't want to be bothered with the facts. It's like the man who won't ask for directions. No, he's a man, so he'll drive around for hours until he figures out where he is. It's the kind of attitude that we—and by that I mean all contractors—have to drop. We have to educate ourselves continually about the best products and the best way of doing things.

How do we prep a subfloor for tiles the right way? There are a number of ways we can go at this. If the substrate is ⅝" OSB, then you have to put at least another ⅝" on top if you choose to tile directly on wood. But always remember that the kitchen, like the bathroom, should be as watertight as possible. WonderBoard and Hardiboard, two concrete-based boards, would do well in place of conventional plywood; they should be set onto the existing subfloor with thinset and then screwed to the subfloor. And it wouldn't hurt to put a waterproof membrane on top of that. My personal favorite is the Ditra product, from Schluter, because not only does it help with watertightness, it actually protects your tiles. It's a bright orange waffled material that is put down right before laying the tile. Even though it's modern, it was designed on the basis of a centuries-old practice. If you look in an old church or school with a stone floor, you'll see that even after more than a 100 years, the stone is probably still almost perfect, with few cracks in it. That's because it's laid on a 2-inch bed of sand. Ditra acts the same way. Like sand, it allows a little bit of flex, a little bit of movement under

Tile floor done right

To install a tile floor properly, you need the right materials and the know-how. Ditra waterproof membrane is the first layer (top left), then take your time laying out your tiles in a consistent pattern (top right). Apply a layer of thinset mortar to the membrane (bottom left), and then wipe the tiles clean before the mortar dries (bottom right).

the finished floor, but the tiles and grout won't crack. Ask your contractor to use this product, or something comparable, for a really good tile floor that will last.

Before we leave the topic of flooring, let me make another important point: Your flooring material should always go under the cabinets, never just to the point where the floor meets the cabinets. This is not an extravagance—it is very important. Your cabinets and appliances are designed to be at a certain height, and that height will always be measured from the finished floor, not from the subfloor. Appliances will not slide in or out of place properly unless they are resting on the finished floor. And if water ever leaks down under the cabinets and you've not floored under them, you're not going to know about that leak unless it floods enough to run downstairs. The water won't run out along the kitchen floor—it will go down under the flooring material. Finally, remember that running the flooring under your cabinets will give you a much cleaner, more pleasing look. Spend more now to do it right.

Step Eight: Cabinets: Choosing Efficient, Durable Storage

When it comes to kitchen cabinets, you'll probably be focused on what they look like. But like everything else in a truly great kitchen, your cabinets should both look good and be built to last. The big question is, do you want custom cabinets or stock cabinets? There's a huge difference between them, more than a lot of people know. And there are pros and cons, of course, to each choice.

Stock cabinets are much cheaper. They are usually made of veneer over particleboard or something similar. Sometimes the doors are solid wood, which will make them look almost custom. These cabinets come in a

multitude of sizes, with base cabinets (the floor-mounted cabinets that the counter sits on) normally 24 inches deep by 34 1/2 inches high. Stock wall cabinets (uppers) would be 12 inches deep by 30 inches high. Widths of both base and upper cabinets can vary from 9 to 48 inches, and generally they increase in 3-inch increments. They might not be a perfect fit, but they can be made to work with a lot of kitchen layouts. Simply by the nature of how they are made, you should save money by using manufactured stock cabinets. Another advantage of is how quickly you can get them—sometimes the same day if you buy them from a big box store.

Which brings us to the biggest issues with custom cabinets. You should be prepared, if they're truly custom, to pay more than you would for stock. How much more? Up to three times as much, roughly. With custom, you're talking about an individual (or several people) taking the time to build your cabinets in their own workshop. And that brings us to the second issue: You must be prepared to wait. Remember that I told you to slow down? Here is one area where you really have no choice. When you order custom cabinets from a good firm, delivery usually takes from six to 12 weeks, and sometimes more. The good firms are usually busy, and building cabinets properly and carefully, from scratch, cannot be rushed. But that's okay, if your planning is good. Settle on your design, order your cabinets, and schedule the actual work on the kitchen for the time when the cabinets will be ready.

I personally love custom cabinets. They're stronger and better designed. They often feature heavier hinges, drawer slides, and other working parts. Custom cabinets will last far longer than any manufactured cabinet. Plus they're created specifically for your kitchen, taking into account your needs and indulging your wildest whims. You can add in an under-counter chopping block, or have a cabinet specifically made to fill some odd nook or cranny. The list of potential materials is almost unlimited, too: oak or maple or cherry—whatever you want, with the finish of your choice. As a bonus, you are usually dealing with people who have had years and years of experience in the kitchen cabinet industry. They really know how to build and install cabinets. That's key.

That brings us to an issue that most people don't understand. So many times I see kitchen companies specifying—right in their contract—a "custom kitchen" or "custom cabinets," but what they put in are stock cabinets. Anyone can open a business saying they do "custom kitchens." Then Joe Builder will design a kitchen for you, fly to a big box store, put together the cabinets, and install them at your house. Joe Builder may appear to be a professional kitchen person, but he's probably not. The money—and, even more, the time you must wait—will tell you if it's really custom.

Step Nine: Adding the Counters and Backsplash

One big idea in kitchen design today is having countertops of differing heights, depending on how you plan to use different areas of the kitchen. I have no issues with different heights for countertops. It looks great. And to me, it's the choice of the homeowner.

The bigger question is the material that you can use on those countertops: granite or stone, which are very popular right now; stone veneer or stone composites; engineered products such as Corian; porcelain or ceramic tile; plastic laminates over particleboard; concrete; stainless steel; butcher block—you name it.

Get what you want with custom cabinets

Real custom cabinets are made to order (top). They often feature better-quality hardware (middle) and allow you to add your own features, like a built-in wine rack (bottom).

Plumb and level is key for cabinet installations

If your contractor doesn't take the time to make absolutely certain that all the cabinets are put in absolutely level and plumb, the boxes won't fit together correctly. Plus, there's the chance that the drawers and doors won't open, close, and operate just right.

What concerns me, always, is the functionality behind the material.

Forget for a moment what your dream counter material looks like. When we talk countertops, we have to start somewhere else: first and foremost, by understanding porous versus non-porous materials. This is critical because you always want to keep your kitchen clean. When you're handling food, cleanliness is a health issue as well as an aesthetic one—bacteria such as salmonella, which can spread from improperly handled poultry products, can make your whole family very, very sick. If you have a countertop that is porous, not only will it stain easily, it will hold germs and bacteria, too. What materials are porous? Surprisingly—because it's so dense and shiny-looking—stone is a big problem in this area. Granite, the number-one choice for countertops, is extremely porous. So are most slates, limestone, soapstone—basically any of the popular natural stones that people are using for counters today, with only a couple of exceptions.

Like any stone counter, granite is sealed with a finish after installation. So, yes, you can clean the counter by wiping it with a cloth if raw chicken or anything else carrying pathogens has made contact with it. The sealant keeps the bacteria from going through into the stone, as long as you wipe it up. But that coating will wear out over time, and that is just with the wear from standard daily cleaning. Take a hot pot off the stove and put it on a granite countertop, and you've lost the seal immediately—that area is now porous. The usual recommendation is that you reapply the sealant once a year, and more often in the most heavily used areas.

► ► ► **Growing quickly in popularity these days are concrete countertops.** People seem to love concrete, perhaps because it can be almost any color and can take great finishes. But concrete, again, is extremely porous. As a matter of fact it's so porous, it's literally like a sponge: It will absorb everything that touches it. Just like granite, it needs to be sealed—every two years at an absolute minimum. It's just as expensive as granite (and sometimes more), plus, as it cures over time, cracks are going to appear and they just can't be repaired easily. Concrete is trendy as all get out, but is it practical? Is it worth installing? In my opinion, no, it's not.

Now if you ask a kitchen company if a particular countertop is porous, they probably won't know enough to tell you the full answer. They're going to say, "Of course it's not porous—we put a finish on this countertop." How long does that finish last? Find out. Trends are fine, but you have to understand what you're purchasing—the good points and the bad.

Let's talk for a second about ceramic or porcelain tile countertops, which are still a popular choice. Tiles are non-porous, they look great, and a tile counter can be cost-effective in comparison to a lot of other materials. The problem comes with the grout. Nine times out of 10, grout is porous, and it will absorb whatever is spilled on it. You will no doubt hear that you simply need to apply a sealant on the grout. This will stop moisture penetrating—for a time. If you're going to do a countertop out of ceramic tile, you're going to want an epoxy mix in your grout, and the system must be made watertight. Your contractor can use plywood and Schluter's Ditra system. There are also trim kits for corners, where the wall meets the counter, which is where cracks always appear in the grout. Best of all is epoxy grout (one of the few places I recommend it) with a waterproof membrane underneath.

Comparing COUNTERTOPS

Material	Water resistance	Cost	Environmental concerns	Good to know	Recommended by Mike?
Butcher block	No	Moderate to high	Uses natural and renewable resources	Wood has natural anti-bacterial properties	Yes
Ceramic or porcelain tile	Yes—but not the grout; must be sealed	Moderate	Uses renewable resources	Installation must be absolutely watertight	Yes
Concrete	No—must be sealed frequently	High	Uses natural and renewable resources	Fine cracks will appear over time, breaking the seal and trapping bacteria	No
Granite, slate,	No—must be sealed frequently	High	Uses natural but non-renewable resources	Once seal has worn off these are among the most porous surfaces	Yes, if maintained
Plastic laminate	Yes	Low	Manufacturing process is not environmentally friendly	Must be well sealed around faucets and sinks to prevent water damage to particle-board core	Yes
Quartz composite	Yes	Moderate to high	Manufacturing process is not environmentally friendly, though some natural materials are used	One of the most durable and non-porous countertops available	Best choice
Solid-surface material	Yes	High	Manufacturing process is not environmentally friendly	Available in almost any color or pattern	Best choice
Stainless steel	Yes	High	Manufacturing process is not environmentally friendly	Easily scratched; does not stain but does show fingerprints	No

This is extremely important, because you don't want the headaches of floods, and you don't want to have to make an insurance claim.

▶ ▶ ▶ **What is the smartest countertop to buy?** There are a few choices on the market that are extremely non-porous. One indicator of a really safe, non-porous material is whether it is approved for use in commercial kitchens or laboratories. Stainless steel falls into this category, and it's also somewhat trendy. It certainly is non-porous, making it easy to keep clean of pathogens. But it shows fingerprints galore and can easily pick up scratches (though some would say that the scratches are part of a "patina" that develops on stainless steel, much like wood or stone that wears over many years). As far as cost is concerned, it's on a par with granite or stone.

Butcher-block countertops are another option, especially for serious cooks. They can be pricy, but they're wonderful for cutting on and you can sand away scratches every few years if you like. Wood also has natural antibacterial properties, which makes it one of the cleanest and safest surfaces for preparing food. A good butcher-block counter can last for many years. They aren't a good idea in a sink area, however.

You can get countertops that will do the job right, from the point

Quartz composite countertops are durable and non-porous. They can look like granite and marble, but are relatively maintenance-free.

Countertops need diligent sealing

There's always lots of water around countertops, whether they are in the kitchen or bathroom. Before the countertop is set in place, it needs to be bedded in beads of high-quality silicone caulk, especially around the sinks. In the bottom right photo, an undermount sink is clamped in place while the silicone caulk (seen in the large center photo) cures.

Although some countertops have a built-in backsplash, I think tile is a good choice for backsplashes. Just be sure to have the joint where the wall meets the countertop sealed with silicone caulking.

of view of both looks and functionality. If you want the look of granite or some other type of stone, check out the different types of composites that are made up of quartz particles bound together with acrylic or epoxy. One type even has built-in protection that will kill microbes. These are among the few products that I know of that have the look of stone or granite but are 100% non-porous and always will be. They don't need a sealant and are virtually maintenance-free.

What about today's solid surfacing materials, such as Corian and its competitors? They are non-porous, quite durable, and available in a huge array of colors and styles that can imitate natural materials. They're quite similar to the quartz countertops just mentioned.

Before we leave counters behind, we need to look at plastic laminates. These are all 100% non-porous, fairly

durable, available in a wide variety of colors and styles, and much cheaper than any other counter option. The drawback is that they are easily scratched or damaged by hot pots, and there's no way to fix those areas. They are also—as I stated earlier—vulnerable to water damage and mold if any part of the particleboard under the laminate comes in contact with water. However, if you use these counters carefully and make sure sinks and faucets have been well sealed where they come in contact with the counter, you can eliminate most of the drawbacks associated with them.

Many countertops—of just about any style—come with a built-in backsplash, or at least the option for it. I suggest doing without it. Counters look great when they're kept nice and flat, meeting the wall at a clean 90-degree angle. Use tile for a backsplash—tile installed over a high-quality, waterproof concrete board, for real durability. Make sure your contractor finishes the job with a bead of caulking where the counter and wall tile meet. This will keep moisture and dirt from building up in that crevice, and it won't crack in the corner the way grout would.

By all means, go ahead and create the wildest kitchen you can imagine, one that will delight your family and wow your friends, or help you make money if the day comes when you want to sell—a room where you can not only cook and eat, but spend many happy hours. But focus on the fundamentals. Get those right, and everything else will feel like a breeze.

CHAPTER SEVEN
Basements

The basement may be underground, but the sky's the limit

You can do a lot with a basement. Just imagine it as a great home entertainment center—you can probably picture the gas fireplace in one corner, the wet bar in another, the big-screen TV ... What a fantastic place to hang out or to entertain your friends. Or maybe it could be a place for the kids to play without driving you crazy and leaving their stuff all over the house. Or how about creating a separate apartment for an older parent, maybe, or to bring in some extra money? Maybe you want some combination of all these possibilities? My company once did a $115,000 basement that had it all: three bedrooms, a kitchen, bathroom, hot tub, and game room, with in-floor heating throughout. It was a work of art. The basement may be underground, but the sky's the limit. > > >

10 things to remember about your
BASEMENT RENOVATION

- Permits: Get them. A typical basement renovation will require four: structural, electrical, plumbing, and HVAC.

- Make sure you're there for all building inspections. Usually there are two stages to the inspection: the rough-in and the final. Be at both.

- If you are lowering a floor, carefully check out the company that will be doing the underpinning—you don't want to mess around here.

- If you are thinking about turning a basement into a separate apartment, check with your local zoning regulations to ensure you're allowed to and be prepared for additional requirements to meet the fire code.

- A bedroom in the basement needs—by law—a window that's large enough for someone to escape in the event of fire. The size of the required window may vary from one municipality to another.

- The best time to add extra wiring for cable TV, telephones, stereos, and computers is before the drywall is up.

- A suspended ceiling with ceiling tiles is usually the best option for basement ceilings, as it allows easy access to wiring, plumbing, and heating ducts.

- If you are enclosing your forced air furnace in a utility room, make sure it has adequate combustion for the operation of the burners.

- Most building codes require a minimum ceiling height of 84 inches for habitable rooms. Some local codes allow some minor variances.

- If you are thinking about screwing wooden strapping to the concrete foundation walls in your basement to save time and money: Don't. You're asking for mold problems, since concrete can get wet, which can rot wood. Wood should never touch concrete. Do it right. Before putting up wooden studs, use rigid styrofoam insulation on concrete foundation walls to create a thermal break.

Many people think that redoing the basement is much like redoing a bathroom or a kitchen. It's not. Before you start, you must understand that basements—because they are below ground level—are different from the main and upper floors of your house. Yes, you still need to follow all the steps you would in other parts of the house—from detailed planning and design through to careful attention to finishes—but first the basement needs to be protected from the hazards of moisture and mold.

In every chapter, it seems, I come back to the Two Commandments of Mike Holmes: Make it watertight, but let it breathe. Basements are the same, only more so. They are surrounded by moisture in the ground on all four sides and underneath, making water infiltration a constant threat. Before you can turn your basement into a usable space, you must deal with that, both inside and out.

Throughout this book, I have talked about slowing down, taking the time to educate yourself and plan wisely. With a basement you must be very clear, right from the start, about what you want. If it's a family room, that's one thing. But if you want that family room to become an apartment later on, you must understand that it will be a lot more work. The good thing about starting a basement renovation is that most basements start out unfinished, which makes it fairly simple to move ahead with just about any plan. Get it straight in your mind what you want from this space. If you do that, and if you take the time to understand the basement, you can make it into usable, finished space for just about any purpose. So let's get started by looking at the various components that make up the basement.

Windows

Windows may seem an odd place to start, but in basements they are more than a finishing detail. Dealing with windows here involves a number of issues, including structure and drainage—it's not the same as putting in a window in an upper level. And looking at windows will give you some idea of the challenges inherent in making a basement into a livable space.

If you want to put a bedroom in the basement, you will almost certainly need a larger window than your basement currently has. By code, builders need put in no more than the minimum, and if your older house was built with an unfinished basement (as almost all are), the builder might

Be clear right from the start about what you want in your basement, now and in the future.

Mike's TIP

Permits required

Basement renovations are different from others you might do, but they do share at least one thing with bathroom and kitchen renovations: You need permits.

Some contractors will tell you that you don't need a permit to do a basic rec room. Wrong. Any wiring changes will still need an electrical permit. That wet bar, or a basement bathroom? A plumbing permit. Putting up walls? Digging down to get more headroom? You'll need a building permit.

If you want to create a little apartment down there—which may include a major rerouting of the HVAC, with separate controls, separate electrical, separate plumbing—then you'll probably need even more. Any bedroom, bathroom, or kitchen in a basement must meet all the minimum code requirements that apply in the rest of your home. An "emergency escape and rescue opening" is required in all basements and bedrooms, which means a window big enough for someone to climb through. You must also have arc fault breakers in those rooms. If you're thinking rental, don't avoid these safety requirements. If anything ever happened in the future in this basement, such as a fire in which someone died, you could be sued—not to mention how awful you would feel.

Another cautionary note: It's not always legal to add a separate apartment unit. Some municipal zoning by-laws don't allow you to rent a second unit in a single-family residence, and sometimes your mortgage will contain a clause stating that your house will never be used as anything other than a single-family home. Before you turn your basement into a rental suite, check it out with an experienced real estate lawyer.

just have installed the smallest possible window. An "emergency escape and rescue opening" is now required in all basements, even unfinished. For a bedroom, by law you need a big enough window for someone to get out in a fire. If you're thinking of using that finished basement space for an office or playroom, you don't need a larger window, but is it wise to put in a larger window anyway? The answer is yes. If you're going to finish your basement for any purpose, you should have a fire escape. Think of people needing to get out or get rescued in case of a fire. Think of your kids. Never assume you can get out another way.

Upgrading to a larger window brings issues. It isn't just a simple matter of cutting a bigger hole in the wall—it means adding a lintel (the horizontal piece that spans the top of the window), new framing, a new window, a window well, and perforated pipe down to the footing. Also, keep in mind that many municipalities require an engineer's evaluation for modification made to concrete or masonry foundations. There is no code method for installing a lintel, so it must be engineered.

You're looking at probably six to 10 times the cost of replacing a window anywhere else in the house. You need to budget for this cost if you're planning to finish your basement.

Let's look more closely at what makes this so expensive. In a new building, the small basement windows are probably above grade, which means they do not require a window well. But if you're going to put in a larger window, you'll probably have to go below grade, and that will require a window well. This is complicated. It means you must dig that area down to the footing and put in a protected vertical perforated pipe system with stone so that any water in the window well gets directed down to the perforated pipe at the bottom. The vertical drainage system will carry the water away, but installing that system means more money.

Suppose, though, that your home already has window wells. Are they done right? Is there a vertical tie-in to the exterior perforated pipe system? Odds are, no, and yet you need this, or the earth will trap water around your windows rather than allowing it to filter down. If you get a quick flood, or even a heavy downpour, it's going to come in through your window. To work properly, the window well must collect water and bring it down to the perforated pipe, away from the window, and away from the house.

Just as important is the lintel, that horizontal piece above the window. I've seen too many contractors pull out a window, cut a bigger hole, and stick a new window in without a structural lintel over it. Without a lintel, that new window bears the weight of the house pushing down on it. Something's going to happen. No one's going to die, but it's going to cost you money, that I can tell you. As a homeowner, you must make sure your contractor does this right.

A River Runs Through It

In Chapter 3, "Inside Your House 101," I talked about getting the basement right. We talked about the signs of problems—efflorescence on the walls, for example, or obvious water damage to the drywall. Obviously, we don't want water in our basement, especially if we have big plans to use it as living space. So what does it

mean to get the basement right?

You're going to hear a lot of contractors and a lot of foundation specialists say that they can put in an interior drainage system. Here's how it works. They dig a narrow trench in the basement between 6 and 8 inches deep, along the perimeter wall, and put a corrugated plastic perforated pipe into it. They cover the pipe with gravel, then with concrete, and the tile gathers up water from the base of the walls and empties it into a sump well. A sump pump carries the water out of the sump and outside the house through a plastic pipe.

In most areas, when you have an interior drainage, you must have a sump pump. (Make sure you check this out with your local building department.) In fact, nowadays, any time you upgrade your basement into a livable space of any kind, you'll likely be required to have a sump well and a sump pump to empty it. The thinking is that it would prevent leaky basements—and expensive insurance claims. It's a simple fix, but there are a couple of problems with it. What happens is that a contractor will install the pump and piping to get the water out of the basement, and then he'll run

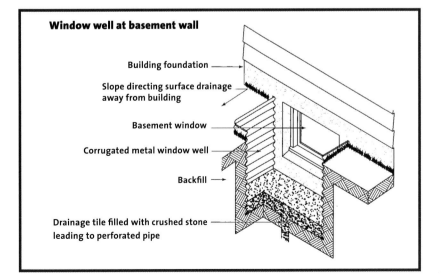

Window well at basement wall

Building foundation

Slope directing surface drainage away from building

Basement window

Corrugated metal window well

Backfill

Drainage tile filled with crushed stone leading to perforated pipe

Concrete seems incredibly solid, but one thing you must understand is that concrete is not waterproof

the pipe so that it sticks out from the exterior wall by only 8 inches. So the water is pumped out and drops down right next to your foundation—where it flows through the wall again, back into the sump pump, and back out. It creates a continuous cycle of pumping. The proper way is to make sure that the drainage pipe empties at least 12 feet away underground and directly into a dry well. Or into a dry pit, which is three to four times the size of the sump pit and filled with stone. This way, the water gets pumped farther away from your home and doesn't come back to the foundation. If you're going to go with an interior drainage system tied to a sump pump, make sure it's run to a dry pit. Never listen to anyone who says anything else, unless you want the water to cycle back through your home over and over again.

The second problem is with the walls. Because the perforated pipe is on the inside of the house (rather than on the outside of the foundation), the walls of your basement are still going to hold a lot of moisture. You're trying to control the water after it has come in. That's key. And I don't like that, especially if you're going to finish the basement. What is that moisture going to do to the drywall? Or to your floors? Remember what I said about building from the outside in? An interior drainage

system can seem very attractive. To be sure, there are plenty of homes where space is really tight around the exterior (where other houses are built very close, for example, or a paved driveway stands between you and the foundation), and in these cases it's a hassle—and an expensive one, at that—to get down to the exterior foundation to do the work. But before you do any of the "finishing" of your basement, make sure to stop the moisture where it's most easily done—outside the foundation walls. Honestly, spend the money. Do it right, or pay for your "economizing" in the future.

So you can see that when it comes to trying to control water with internal drainage systems and sump pumps, I am usually opposed. That said, there are a couple of sound applications for internal drainage systems. John McRae of McRae Foundations, who has done foundation work for us on the show, will put in an interior perforated–pipe system whenever he lowers a basement floor—but this is when he has moved the foundation down, beneath the depth of the exterior perforated pipe.

Another system of interior drainage that I will accept, and even recommend, is for use in new houses only. It's a product called Form-A-Drain. This is made up of long plastic forms, about 8 inches tall, designed as a mold for footings in new homes. But unlike conventional concrete forms, which are wood, these are not taken off after the concrete has hardened. They're left in place. Every 8 feet, they feature a cross-membrane from inside to outside. This allows water gathered internally to flow back outside again, where we want it to be. I highly recommend this system if you're going to do a custom build. But that is the only place it will work—in new building.

The Floor

Water seeping through the foundation walls isn't the only moisture challenge you'll face in your basement. You have to think about the water table, too. What is the water table? Basically, it's the highest underground point at which water saturates the ground. Everywhere in the world there is water stored under the ground, and the water table marks the top of that storage zone. You know that soil is always damp, but if you dig down to the water table, you are looking at a pool of water. It isn't just damp—it's groundwater. The water table can be just a few feet below the surface, and its level can change through the year, with the seasons.

Now, in most houses, old or new, the basement floor is concrete. How those concrete floors were built depends, as with so many components of our houses, on when they were built. The modern method is to lay down four inches of gravel and pour a concrete floor on top. (This is not the way I would do it, and I will talk about that later.) An older house, though, is unlikely to have anything even this elaborate. Originally, the basement might have had a dirt floor, and concrete was put over it later.

Concrete seems incredibly solid, but one thing you must understand is that concrete is not waterproof. Even if there are no visible cracks, water will get through; it's just the nature of the material. And in a basement this is particularly troublesome, because of the water table. When the water table is close to the underside of the concrete floor, water will wick through the concrete.

But that's not the only moisture issue that's associated with the basement floor. If you go six feet deep in the earth—almost anywhere—you'll find the temperature to be about 60 to 68 degrees Fahrenheit, year-round. This has to do with the earth's natural temperature. So if your basement floor is approximately four feet below ground level—and that's normally how deep the floor will be—you will have, at the bottom, a zone where the temperature is always going to be the same, year-round. In the summer, chances are the air above the floor in your basement is going to be warmer than the air that's higher up. Warmer air holds a lot of moisture, and when it hits that cooler basement floor, you get condensation.

Lots of homeowners and contractors just ignore the problem of moisture in a basement floor. In many basements, you will see tile, linoleum, or vinyl laid right on the concrete floor. Bad idea. The adhesive used to put down these floorings is called mastic, and mold loves mastic. To my knowledge, there isn't a mastic out there yet that doesn't promote mold. Put mastic into an area with moisture, and you will get mold, especially if the mastic is covered in vinyl or some other layer that won't let the air get to it.

▶ ▶ ▶ **You must accept that your basement floor is always going to have moisture issues,** and even have different issues at different times of the year. How do you put any kind of floor on top of that and keep it dry?

Flooring manufacturers will tell you to put down a 6-mil plastic sheet vapor retarder on top of the concrete,

and then you can put down anything over that, even an oak floor if you feel like it. This would be a huge mistake. Even if you put a sheet of plastic on top of concrete, moisture will still come up through that concrete—only now you're trapping the moisture on top of the concrete, which can create a surface mold right there between the plastic and the concrete. It's the cheap way, and though it's acceptable according to the building code, you should never do it.

Some people will tell you to get one of those epoxy-based products that you apply directly over your concrete floor. The idea is that these products seal it, filling in all the little dings and cracks and giving you a smart, smooth finish. I don't like this either. In putting some sort of watertight sealer on top of the concrete, you might as well go back to the first option, putting down the 6-mil plastic. No matter which one you choose, you're going to trap the moisture. With the epoxy, you can end up with water pushing up from the floor against the epoxy layer and,

with enough pressure behind the water, this can cause the sealant to fail. For the same reason, never use an oil paint on concrete. In fact, do not seal concrete in any way whatsoever.

What do you need to do? I recommend a combination of rigid foam board, laid right over the concrete, and plywood. This is going to amount to about 1 5/8" of thickness on the floor, before you put down your flooring material, but most new homes have enough height in the basement to allow for that. The contractor will start by putting down 1" rigid foam-board insulation. This can be either what is commonly called pink board, made by Corning, or blue board, available from Dow. It doesn't matter which one is used—both are great products. The foam boards go down over the concrete but are not glued to it. If you glue anything to your basement floor, you are potentially providing mold spores with a material they can eat. So, no glue.

Instead, the crew should apply a low-expansion

spray foam along all the exterior edges—where the flooring meets the walls—and then tape at every single joint. Then, on top of the foam, you want to have ⅝" tongue-and-groove plywood, which should be screwed through the foam and into the concrete floor. This should be done with Tapcon screws, which are designed for concrete—they are expensive, but they are the best screws to use for this job. There is nothing else on the market that will compare.

This works for a perfect floor. After this, you can put any type of flooring you want on top. You can put down carpet or hardwood, or you can put down tile. This base is structurally strong enough to put ceramic or porcelain tile on directly, though I recommend using Ditra as well, which has a cushioning effect that protects the tile. You can even put vinyl right over it and odds are you're not going to get mold. Pretty well any finish that strikes your fancy will work.

Why is it that the foam-board method works? A big reason is that it deals with a problem the plastic sheeting can't solve, which is the constant temperature of the basement floor. The foam is an insulator: It creates a thermal break between the concrete floor and the temperature of the air in the basement, which is constantly changing. This insulation between the two temperatures prevents condensation—and that means no mold.

Let me go back one step and tell you about my perfect concrete floor. This is what I would put in if I could tear up everything that is there and start again. First, I'd put down gravel. You've got to have gravel under the concrete because you need a drainage bed so water can drain away without coming into contact with the concrete. Next, I would recommend a 2-inch layer of

Mike's TIP

Dreaming of wood floors?

Lots of people imagine a finished basement space that looks exactly like any other room in the house—right down to the oak flooring they love for their living room or den. And you can have that, provided you follow every one of the steps to make your basement waterproof. Anything less and you will set up your hardwood flooring for buckling, warping, molding—total failure, not to mention the frustration and expense for you. Make the basement totally watertight, and you can use any finish you like.

Understand, right off the bat, that lowering the floor is more than just digging down

the rigid foam insulation I just spoke of. But in this case, it goes on top of the gravel and ultimately underneath the poured concrete. That way you're creating a thermal break underneath the floor, which will solve our condensation problems, and you're stopping most moisture from coming through. Concrete with foam-board insulation under it is the perfect subfloor for any type of flooring you choose.

Dropping the Floor

In most modern homes, the height of the basement is sufficient to do any finishing you'd like. You take care of the moisture issues on the floor and walls, of course, but you can take your renovation pretty simply from there. But many older homes have a ceiling much lower than you find in houses built today. These old basements have barely six feet of headroom, if that, and this is often taken up with ductwork. I think it was simply assumed that no one would spend any time down there, except for doing the laundry or stoking the old coal furnace. In a house like that, trying to make the basement into a livable space probably requires lowering the floor.

To do this, you're going to see prices ranging from $5,000 to $100,000. I have seen quotes of $30,000 to do basements of only 600 square feet. There's almost no limit to what you can pay for what can be a very complex job. It may require a conveyor belt to carry the dirt out or, if your basement is really hard to excavate, a bucket brigade of workers to bring the dirt out and get the concrete in.

Understand, right off the bat, that lowering the floor is more than just digging down. You're playing with structure. Indeed, you are actually undermining—though only temporarily, you hope—the walls of your home. This work requires a permit. Don't duck this, and don't listen to (or work with) any contractor who tells you to duck it. The contractor is responsible for the job only until he leaves, and then you're left holding the bag. Sure, he's legally responsible if anything goes wrong. But think: Do you want to get a lawyer and go after him down the road?

Making a basement deeper is a very tricky process. You have to do what is called underpinning. That means, before lowering the floor, creating a new footing (the widest part of the foundation, which the walls sit on) for the foundation underneath the existing one. If you were to ignore this and just dig the floor down below the level of the footing, you would actually weaken the structure of the wall. If the foundation wall was not sitting right in the middle of the footing but was off to one side or the other, it could shift and start to give way.

To do this properly, working within building codes and with permits, you have to go very slowly. The idea is to dig down underneath the footing, getting down to undisturbed soil. Then you create a cradle of some sort and pour some concrete into it to extend your footings down to the new floor depth. When this has set, you can move on to do another three feet section, then another, then another. Go any faster, and you compromise the foundation.

Even going slowly, though, problems can show up after the concrete has been poured. First, new concrete does not adhere to old, set concrete. And because the new concrete is going to shrink as it dries, there is going to be a gap and the possibility of movement between the new footing and the old. You must use a non-shrinkable grout between the new footing and the old to create a continuous support. This is called a bridging, a footing, or an underpinning, depending on how you do it. Whatever method is used, there must be about an inch of non-shrinkable grout tucked right back underneath the full width of the original footing. Frequently, though, that grout won't go right to the back, and even an inspector won't see the problem: If the first few inches are completely sealed, he can't see past them. But having that gap completely filled is critical, because not doing so will compromise the structure of your home. You're going to have a breakable foundation—and you won't even know it until something happens.

There are new products for filling this gap on the

Extra caution required!

There are a lot of companies out there that try to take on jobs they've never done before. For some reason—maybe because they can charge so much—underpinning is one of them. I have actually seen an underpinning job that nearly ended in catastrophe. In this case, they dug down below the level of the flooring for the full length of the foundation wall. The structure cracked. The city slapped a stop-work order and a homeowner removal order on the house. The company that did this was very lucky the whole house didn't cave in. The lesson? Be extra careful to check references and experience for any contractor who'll be working on your foundation.

Here's where most contractors go wrong, because they're treating the basement like any other part of the house

market right now. One of them was developed by John McRae. McRae gets right underneath the existing footing and creates a U-shaped trough that cups the old footing from underneath. Concrete is poured in and then vibrated so that it settles into place right underneath the old footing and up the other side of it, holding it tightly in place. This method is engineer-approved, and it works. It does away with the whole problem that the non-shrinkable grout is supposed to fix but too often doesn't.

It's important to understand that underpinning shouldn't just stop with the basement. If your basement has a door to the outside with, typically, concrete stairs leading down to it, that area will need to be underpinned, too. Most contractors will tell you they don't need to touch those stairs. Not so. The stairs, walls, and floor of that entry stairwell must be lowered. In fact, the foundation walls of that entrance must be even lower than the new floor—they must go down four feet lower. This means digging down and putting in a new structure all the way up. If you have a walk-in basement, your underpinning could cost you twice as much as just doing the inside. This is definitely

something to think about.

Underpinning is a radical procedure, and an expensive one. To be honest, as a way of gaining space it may be more expensive than it's worth. I'm not saying it can't be done—in a renovation anything is possible—but you definitely need to think about it carefully beforehand. If your basement requires this sort of work, an addition may be an easier and potentially cheaper way to gain more space.

On to the Walls

The single biggest mistake that I see in basement renovations is the way the walls are insulated, and again this has to do with the constant temperature at floor level and on the parts of the walls that are below ground. Let me explain. In the first and second floor of your home, you are allowed to have air movement behind your drywall. You can use batt insulation that air can move through. Why is this? Because the air temperature in those walls is the same from top to bottom. Not from one side of the wall to the other, obviously—that's why you need a vapor retarder on the warm side of the wall. But top to bottom of the walls upstairs, the temperature is pretty constant.

In the basement, it's a completely different story. There's a constant temperature at ground level but variable temperatures the farther up you go from the ground. It gets complicated by the fact that—no surprise—there isn't a foundation wall out there that is exactly vertical, exactly plumb. And on top of that, because moisture can always wick through the walls, just like the floor, you don't ever want the wood studs to be attached directly to the walls.

How do most contractors solve these problems? The standard way of finishing a studded wall in the basement is to bring the studs out approximately one inch or even more from that wall. But here's where most contractors go wrong, because they're treating the basement like any other part of the house: They will insulate in between each and every stud and put up 6-mil vapor barrier, which is minimum code. And it's all fine, or appears to be fine. But in fact, as long as those studs are one inch away from the wall—and remember this is an outside wall—there will be air movement. Why? Well, we know we have a zone of constant temperature at the bottom. In the winter, that means air that is warmer than the outside air. The warm air will rise up that wall and, where the foundation is above ground, it will hit a cold zone. When warm meets cool, what happens? Condensation. And what does that create? Mold. Because condensation is now trapped in behind the wall and will stay there behind the vapor barrier, mould will thrive and the wood will rot. So how do we stop that?

When framing a basement wall the wood should never sit directly on a concrete floor. A foam layer protect the wood from moisture.

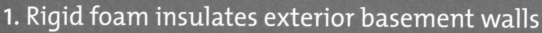

1. Rigid foam insulates exterior basement walls

The right way to finish a basement wall. Glue rigid foam to the exterior foundation wall (top left), tape the seams (top right), and seal the gaps with foam (bottom).

2. After the foam comes the framing

Building a stud wall in a basement (left and top right). Once you've framed the wall, you can insulate (bottom right). You don't need to use a vapor barrier with a rigid foam break.

You can have the basement of your dreams. How? By making it dry and breathable.

Some contractors will tell you to use metal studs. Put them right against the wall, and don't leave an air space. No, sorry. Put metal studs against that uneven exterior wall, and you're still going to have air movement. You're still going to get condensation. What's more, it will rust like crazy, because it's in a moist area, thanks to the condensation. There's something else, too—metal is a much better conductor of hot and cold than wood. That zone behind the wall is cold. The metal stud will transmit the cold right through to the inside. Warm air, cold stud—now you're looking at condensation. Within five years you will be able see where every one of those drywall screws is. They will rust right out. Do not use metal studs on an exterior wall. If you do, you're spending your money incorrectly. The only place in your basement to consider using metal studs is in an interior wall.

What's the best solution? For me, it's to use rigid 2" foam (up to 2⅝") on the outside walls—the same sort of pink or blue board you put on the floor, only thicker, using the proper adhesive for foam board. Glue spots every 12 inches and leave about a quarter-inch gap all the way around the perimeter of each board, and fill it with spray foam to seal the boards together and stop any air movement in the corners. Then tape all the seams. You want no air movement. So, you've created that thermal break on the inside, and that means you don't need plastic sheeting as a vapor barrier. Then you frame the walls, which allows you to create a nice plumb surface, which you could not do if you tried gluing the drywall to the insulation. The space between the drywall and the insulation board also gives you room to run wiring, plumbing, and HVAC. Keep in mind that the basement is another place where you want to have mold-proof drywall, as you do in your bathroom and kitchen.

With this method, you've stopped air movement, and below ground that is a good thing—not just for preventing condensation, but for reducing fire hazard, something that most people aren't even aware of when finishing a basement. Fire needs three things: an ignition source, flammable material, and air. Suppose you have the usual setup of air movement behind the wall and insulation with plastic sheeting as a vapor barrier. Now suppose an electrical receptacle sparks. There's your ignition source. The plastic sheeting vapor barrier is a material where fire can start. And the air behind the wall will feed

Properly finished basements can be used for anything—including a playroom for the kids.

the fire. Foam-board insulation is non-combustible, so you've removed the flammable material. The more we can eliminate fire hazards, water hazards, and moisture hazards, the better off we are.

Getting Down to the Dream

Once you have done any necessary window enlargements and have sealed the floors and the walls (the work on walls and floors should be done at the same time), you are ready to start creating your dream basement. What your contractor has done is to create a virtual container (like a picnic cooler) that will keep out moisture, stop condensation, and feel warm and snug. And because of properly sized and supported windows and doors, you'll be able to get out of it in case of an emergency. With that container made dry but breathable, you can start filling it up. It's a sign of how different basements are from the rest of the house that so much work must be done before even starting on what most of us would think of as the renovation.

Basement Bathrooms

Most brand-new homes nowadays have what is called a rough-in for a bathroom in the basement. This consists of hot and cold lines, a toilet drain, and a drain prepared for a shower with a ventilation line. Most often, unfortunately, the rough-in is in the wrong spot. New-home builders will throw in a rough-in anywhere—beside the furnace, under the ductwork. It doesn't matter to them because it's really all about selling something extra to you.

If your basement has a rough-in, that at least means you have a proper vent line. That means air behind water, and you can tie into that in a more convenient location.

The toilet should be within five feet of that stack, but what kind of a bathroom can you create so close to the furnace? You're probably going to wind up running a line right through your house, right through the roof. Be prepared for this. Find a zone that you can run through—maybe an upstairs closet, if you have to—but make sure that the contractor does it, because otherwise you're going to have problems with your basement bathroom.

Apart from that issue, a basement bathroom is no different than upstairs. It must be watertight, it must be mold-free, it must be done correctly. There are special challenges—you may have to break through concrete to run pipes and put in drains—but challenges like this are manageable.

If you don't have a rough-in, which would be the case for the majority of older homes, where do you tie for the vent? You simply have to install a new 3" line directly up to the attic and out the roof. It's not as hard as it sounds and just a little money more.

Heating and Ventilation

Even if the basement is heated (e.g. ductwork, radiators, or baseboard heat), you'll probably need to make some changes when you renovate. As soon as you close up the areas by putting in partition walls and creating rooms, you've changed airflow. You will need an HVAC permit, and—to really do things right—you'll need to bring in an HVAC expert. To bring heat down from the ceiling (it will naturally rise) and to create proper airflow, you need expert advice.

If air goes in, air must come out: It's a question of finding the balance. And that's what an expert will tell you how to do. In most cases you can get away with one air return for the basement, but if the experts say you need an extra air return in a particular place, you must put one in.

You probably won't have to upgrade your furnace to do a basement renovation. This is because you'll be insulating walls that really were not properly insulated in the first place. But a new furnace—a higher-efficiency one, possibly—is something you might want to think about. This is the time to make the change. The same with a new tankless water heater, and maybe switching over to PEX piping. Or upgrading your electrical. If you are already down there in the basement, now is your chance.

One thing I would do in any basement renovation is to create a utility room that has everything: the plumbing manifold, the tankless hot water system, the high-efficiency furnace, the electrical breaker box. Create that utility room so that it's well set up, and leave it unfinished, so that in the future you can add in anything extra you need.

The Ceiling

Once you have the floor and the walls sorted out and you have made it snug and dry, finishing the basement is pretty much like working on any other part of the house. There's one other exception—the ceiling. Should you drywall the ceiling or install a suspended ceiling? If you asked all the contractors out there, you'd probably find opinion split at about 50-50. Let's look at the pros and cons.

For head clearance, drywalling the ceiling gives you more height. A suspended ceiling means you will lose about three inches of headroom. For many people, a drywalled ceiling is the preferable one in terms of looks—it just looks more finished, more like rooms in any other part of the house. With suspended ceilings,

there are a variety of ceiling tiles available, however, some of them quite attractive-looking. And if you go with a suspended ceiling, you should spend the extra money on something that looks nice.

The major advantage of a suspended ceiling is that it allows accessibility. It lets you get to electrical junctions in the ceiling, for instance, an important consideration because you should never hide a junction point of electricity. At any time in the future, you can get into the floor joists to run phone lines, cable lines, or speaker lines. A suspended ceiling may save you money in the end because you won't have to deal with the junctions or other systems, such as plumbing, that run through that space, in the same way as you would if you drywalled the ceiling. Also, if a flood upstairs in your kitchen or bathroom drips down to the basement ceiling, you'll just need to change a couple of tiles rather than repair drywall. Looks and added headroom with drywall, vs. the accessibility factor of suspended ceilings—you must weigh the costs and benefits.

You can have the basement of your dreams. How? By making it dry and breathable. Waterproofing from the outside. Using the proper products and techniques. If you and your contractor can do those things right the first time, you'll enjoy your renovated basement for years to come, without repair costs in the future. You'll pay once, not twice.

CHAPTER EIGHT

The Home Stretch

Make sure that all the small details have been taken care of with your contractor

Whenever we finish a project on HOLMES ON HOMES or HOLMES INSPECTION, there's always a great moment at the end of the show. It's when we bring the people we've helped back into their home and they see their fixed-up house for the first time after having gone through all that financial distress and worry about how to fix it. The homeowners are happy, and I get a hug. In all honesty, the hug is my pay— it's all I need. That might sound odd, but the money really isn't why my crew and I put in long hours redoing botched renovations and taking the time to do things right. We do it because we can help. We can make it right. And hopefully, through the show, we've shown other people how to do it right, too. > > >

Mike's TIP

Signed, sealed, delivered . . .

When I talked about contracts early in the book, I cautioned against setting up a payment schedule that is tied to dates. Never do this! Always gear your payments to work completed. Toward the end of the job, make your list of outstanding items, have the contractor complete the jobs on the list, and then pay him.

Now, I'm lucky that the show pays for me and my crew, but to any good contractor, money is not the only reward. Contractors enjoy being able to help people achieve their dreams: the kitchen they've always wanted, the new rec room for the kids, or the incredible spa bathroom. It doesn't matter what the project is, a good contractor is there with you, excited about doing it right and proud of the final results. That's how you can feel, too, with your renovation nearly complete. But before you sit back and enjoy, it's important to make sure that all the small details have been taken care of with your contractor. On your own, take the time to go through the renovation site and make a list of any items that still need to be done or that you're concerned about. A door doesn't close properly? Some paint touch-ups are needed after the cabinet installation? The list you'll make now (and the discussion you'll have with your contractor) is the best way to ensure that the job is done—fully, completely, and to your total satisfaction.

Here are some questions to ask yourself as you make the list:

►►► Are all appliances in place and in working order? Do you have manufacturer warranties and manuals for new appliances and mechanicals (such as the furnace)?

►►► Are all faucets working properly?

►►► Are all the electrical outlets and switches in the logical spot and at the right height? And check that the right outlets have been installed (like GFCI outlets wherever there are water hazards like bathrooms and kitchens).

►►► Is everything caulked and sealed (around faucets, sinks, toilets, etc.)?

► ► ► Is all cabinet hardware installed securely?

► ► ► Do all doors, windows, and cabinets open easily and smoothly?

► ► ► Is the grout even and neat on new tile floors? Do the floors lie flat, without any protruding corners or edges?

► ► ► Is all molding installed, painted, or stained (including end cuts)?

Go over the list with your contractor until you're in agreement about exactly what must be done, and when. He won't be surprised that you're not planning to pay until the list is complete, and he'll be motivated to get some workers back quickly to finish the job.

Finally, don't sign the last check to your contractor until you have a copy of the contractor's final invoice showing that the amount has been paid in full.

A Stitch in Time

It might seem cruel to bring this up right away, but now that you've done so much work on your house, it's important to maintain it. I know, I know—housework is never done. But you've put a lot of money into your renovation, and you want to protect your investment. That means regularly inspecting your house and taking the necessary maintenance precautions. The good news is that just by making sure your renovation was done properly, with the right materials and techniques, you've already got less to worry about than the average homeowner.

Where do you start? It's a good idea to inspect your house step by step in the fall and spring. Take pictures

of anything that concerns you, especially if you want to track it. Photocopy and follow the checklist on the next page, and trust your gut. And if you're uncomfortable with anything, call in a pro to take a look for another opinion. If it's an issue that relates to a recent renovation, ask your contractor to come back and take a look.

The Big Stuff

The important time for house maintenance is in the fall. Winter can be tough on your house, so in the fall it's important to get your house ready. In the spring you're looking for any damage from the winter. Use the checklist on the next page and pay careful attention to the big stuff, outside and in.

WINDOWS AND DOORS

Check for cracked and missing caulking, and replace it. Take a look at your window sills. This is the sort of flat surface where water can gather and get in. If it's precast concrete, that's good. If it's wood, keep it primed and painted. If it's brick laid side on side, that can let in a lot of water. A simple solution is to buy a can of concrete sealant and just paste it over the area. Don't do the whole wall—we want it to breathe. But here, sealing will help keep that water out.

If your house is wood or has outside wood trim, you want to keep it nicely painted. Scrape it, prime it, and paint it. I can't say how important primer is. Primer, not paint, is what seals the wood against moisture. And, whatever you do, don't use oil paint over it. It traps moisture and doesn't allow your wood to breathe. When moisture becomes trapped behind the oil paint, the wood can expand and contract and cause the paint to pull away from the surface.

A maintenance
CHECKLIST

Take a bit of time twice a year to check over your house. A little bit of maintenance now can pay off in the long term.

FALL

- Check foundation for cracks.
- Check chimney for deteriorated or missing mortar or bricks.
- Check that grading is sloped away from the house.
- Look for any missing, loose, or damaged shingles on your roof.
- Check caulking on flashing.
- Check and clean gutters.
- Make sure downspouts are extended at least 5 feet from the house.
- Check decks, patios, porches, and stairs for signs of loose boards, rot, or decay.
- Check weatherstripping on exterior doors.
- Cover central air-conditioning units.
- Check your sump pump for proper operation.
- Have your forced air furnace serviced by a qualified service company.
- Check all smoke detectors and carbon monoxide detectors.
- If your basement is unfinished, check the walls for any signs of moisture or efflorescence.

SPRING

- Check wood siding and trim for signs of deterioration; clean, replace, or refinish as necessary.
- If you live in an area that is not serviced by a municipality, have your well water tested for quality and safety.
- Turn off the humidifier on your furnace.
- Check fences and deck railings, and repair or replace them if necessary.
- Disconnect the duct connected to your dryer, vacuum the lint from the duct, and clean the dryer's vent hood outside.
- Check and, if necessary, repair window screens.
- Repair any damaged steps that might be a safety hazard.
- Check all smoke detectors and carbon monoxide detectors.

Companies push oil paint, suggesting that you will have less maintenance—that is, less painting—to do. Do not use it, no matter what anyone says. In the long run, you're going to have a lot more to fix. Latex, on the other hand, will allow water vapor to pass through the paint, so it's less likely to peel off if your home has a lot of interior moisture. Latex paint is more flexible than oil-based paint, so it's also less likely to crack.

Make sure your doors to the outside shut tightly. Check the weatherstripping for wear.

THE ROOF

Get up on your roof if you can, because you don't want water getting in. If you're at all nervous, bring in a pro

roofer to do this. In general, you might want every couple of years to get in a roofer to look at your roof, to check the caulking and to look for missing and damaged shingles and any problem with your flashing. You don't want to wait 10 years to call him in—and then find you have to call in someone else to fix the drywall and pull out the insulation that got wet.

PORCH AND STEPS

Do you have a concrete porch? They are pretty common in houses built in the '50s and '60s. If you have cracks in that concrete, fix those cracks. There are all kinds of products you can use—there are waterproofing products and epoxy fill, and at a bare minimum you can use caulking as a temporary

This roof has served its useful life. Cupped, damaged, or missing shingles are a sure sign that an asphalt roof needs replacing.

Mike's TIP

When do you get your roof done?

If you find problems with your shingled roof in the fall and you might need roof replacement, try not to get the work done in the winter. Asphalt shingles are more brittle in the winter. And asphalt shingles might not seal properly in the winter, causing them to suffer wind damage, Also, crews are cold and more likely to cut corners, so you might not end up with as good a job. Talk to your roofing company, and wait if you can. Some roofers may patch your roof for free to get you through the winter if you've signed up for the job in the spring.

fix. Whatever you choose, you want to stop the water from getting in. If that water freezes and then melts repeatedly, your porch will fall apart fast.

Make sure your steps are safe and repair any damaged or broken steps.

GUTTERS AND DOWNSPOUTS

Clean out any leaves in your gutters and make sure they're not clogged with debris. A clogged gutter can cause snow to back up on your roof over a winter. It can tear the gutter—and the fascia board—right off. Make sure that your gutters are connected to your downspouts. Check those downspouts, too. Are they connected into the perforated pipe or other drainage system? Get them out. They should be extended at least 5 feet away from your house or into a rain barrel. But don't put the water down next to your foundation.

FOUNDATION

If you've converted your damp old basement into a dry, livable space, you want to keep it that way. Is your grade running into your house or away from your house? Keep that grade at a minimum 5-degree slope away from your house all the way around your property. What does that mean? You want the ground 10 feet away from your house to be a good 6 inches lower than it is at your foundation. Look at your sidewalk, too. Is your sidewalk sloping into your home? How about your patio stones?

Inside
HEATING SYSTEM

Have your gas or oil furnace checked and serviced by a qualified company every fall. Ensure that their service includes testing your furnace for carbon monoxide. Clean and turn on the furnace humidifier. Service your heat recovery ventilator (HRV), too. And, most important, change the filter in a forced air furnace regularly. A standard furnace requires a filter. Each and every filter needs to be cleaned and replaced as often as possible. If you have an electronic air cleaner, you have to clean it once a month. If you have a HEPA filter, you should replace it every two or three months. I say this is not often enough. For all these filters, once a month would be fabulous—to replace them, not just to clean them. If you want to clean them, clean them twice a month. Never mind this once-or-twice-a-year nonsense.

Why do we want to keep our filters clean and replace them on a regular basis? I'm going to give you the best example of all. In a standard furnace (not a high-efficiency one), the exhaust is attached to the chimney. If you leave an air filter in a furnace too long, the filter gets clogged, blocking the air flow to the furnace from your cold air return. If your furnace starves for air and can't pull the air from where it's supposed to, which is from the cold air return in your home, it starts to pull it from the room that the furnace is in. And if there's not enough air in that room, guess where the furnace pulls air from? From the chimney. It can pull exhaust fumes, notably carbon monoxide, back into your home. That can kill your whole family. How important is a simple filter in a furnace? Deadly important. Keep them clean.

WATER LEAKS

Of course, water isn't a problem only on the outside. In fact, water inside our homes can cause nearly as many problems. Water damage in our bathroom or kitchen may in fact be the reason we had to renovate in the first place.

Changing your furnace filter every month is one of the most important things you can do for safety and energy efficiency.

Let's talk about bathrooms first. What is your No. 1 leak spot? It's usually the shower head or the tub spout or the faucets for the tub. Let's look at the shower head. We have threaded joints in behind there, and if our Teflon tape or whatever other product we are using has worn out over the years, it will slowly drip. This is your No. 1 mold spot. But it's easy to fix. Every couple of years, take off your showerhead, check the area around it, put on new Teflon tape, screw the head back on again, and seal that hole with clear silicone. Do the same with your tub spout. Remove it as well and do an inspection. With the taps, we want to take a caulking gun with clear silicone and put a small bead around the top. You may have seen me do this on the show. Just put a bead along the top, but not underneath. Water is not going to come up from underneath, and if any does penetrate the silicone on the top, we want it to drain right out again. So if you notice a leak on your ceiling underneath your bathroom, odds are it's one of these three—your shower head, your tub spout, or your faucets—or your toilet, because it was installed with a rubber gasket. We always want to use a wax gasket with a plastic ring.

When it comes to faucets for sinks in bathrooms and kitchens, we have to think about splash-out. Depending on how they were installed, splashing can get under the sink and under the faucets and can saturate the countertop underneath the sink. Get underneath to see if the countertop is wet. If it is wet, odds are you've got a water zone that can create rot and mold problems. Remove the faucets, create a seal with silicone or plumber's putty, and put them on again.

This may not sound like much of a maintenance tip, but keep your bathroom clean. The same goes for your kitchen. Clean them as often as you can, but use as little water as you can. Most of the caulking or silicone used in both rooms is not mold-free. We have wonderful clean-freaks in the world who just love to soak things with water, which I do not recommend. Use as little water as possible, and keep your surfaces as dry as possible.

VENTILATION

Now let's talk about breathing again. We want our home to breathe. Think of your home as a set of lungs. If your house doesn't have fresh air coming in, it's not healthy. This is a major problem today. People constantly feel that they're getting a cold, but they might not realize that it could be the air in their home that is making them sick. How much dust do you have in your house? How many people do you have living in your house? Do you have carpeting, dogs, cats? The more movement you have in the home, the more dust you have, the more junk in the air.

I've talked a lot about mold. Do you know that typically there are 18,000 spore counts of mold in fresh air? We're used to breathing this on a daily basis, so it doesn't bother us, but how much more mold do we actually have in our homes? We need good ventilation fans, and we must not be afraid to run them. Let your bathroom fan run at least 30 minutes after a shower, and be sure to use your range hood when you're cooking. They'll help with moisture issues, too.

A Few Last Words

None of these maintenance tips is particularly difficult. They don't require incredible tools or a high degree of knowledge. These are all things most people can do themselves, but you shouldn't hesitate to call in the pros when you need to.

And if you need to have a smaller job done or you're getting the renovation itch again, don't forget that, no matter what size your project is, you must take your time. Treat any job on your home as seriously as you would a major renovation. Don't go with the first guy who shows up. Do your research. Ask for references. Go see his previous work. If you slow down, educate yourself, and hire right, you should always get it right the first time.

Whenever my crew and I can help out homeowners who've gone through a bad renovation, I can see their relief and how happy they are with the finished results. That's a great feeling for us. But imagine how much better it would be if every homeowner learned what you've just learned by reading this book: In a renovation, anything is possible—if you follow the steps to make it right.

ACKNOWLEDGEMENTS

I've always said you are only as good as the people around you.

Fortunately, I'm surrounded by many very talented and supportive people—close family, friends, and colleagues who have helped me make it right for many people. And reaching out to help more people is really what this book is all about.

What you won't see in these pages are the thousands of conversations I've had during more than two decades of contracting. Conversations with terrific contractors who share a passion for their trade and for doing it right the first time; conversations with homeowners who are keen to learn and who respect the skill needed to help turn their house into a home; and conversations with complete strangers of all ages who simply want to share their stories, their curiosity, and their thanks. Each and every one of those meetings has encouraged me, taught me, and occasionally humbled me.

To my right- and left-hand men, Pete Kettlewell and Michael Quast, as well as Lilana Novakovich, and David Dembroski, thanks for being there in my corner and sharing the mission.

To the hundreds of contractors who have helped and continue to help deserving homeowners, thank you. Members of the regular *HOLMES ON HOMES* crew deserve specific mention. From Shawn Morren, who was there at the beginning, to Damon Bennett, Adam Belanger, Steve Buck, Carl Pavlovic, Corin "Pinky" Ames, and Bill Bell, who all stand by me now, thank you. The folks you never see on television, but who help just as much with their skill and dedication, include: from The Holmes Group—Liza Drozdov, Mark Bernardi, Dave Goard, Amanda Heath, Tara Jan, Stephanie Liang, Seth Atkins, Steve Tsushima, Brian Warchol, Richard Wilmot, and Andrew Wood. Also, my thanks to Alliance Atlantis and HGTV Canada for their constant support and encouragement.

To everyone at HarperCollins, including Neil Erickson, Alan Jones, Lloyd Kelly, Nita Pronovost, Iris Tupholme, Brad Wilson, and Noelle Zitzer, many thanks.

Thanks also to Joseph Marranca, Ian Coutts, and Nicole Langlois. And thanks to Michael Afar, Lisa and Jim Blanden, Stephanie Fysh, Karen Hamada, Jack Hoogstraten, Hamad Kamal, Louie Katsis, Stephanie Leupp, Pier Antoine Marier, Jeff Monk, Franca Palmieri, Don Penfold, Bruce Schallenberg, Gillian Watts, and Greg Wells.

Finally, to Anna—thanks for caring so much for so long. And to my three children, Amanda, Sherry, and Mike Jr., you are the reason I keep going. I love you all dearly.

GLOSSARY

A

ABS (acrylonitrile butadiene styrene)
Hard black plastic plumbing pipes, used primarily for drainage. The rule of thumb for drainage pipes is ABS pipes in your house and PVC for in-ground pipes. Some municipalities forbid the use of ABS pipe for any application.

AFCI (arc fault circuit interrupter)
An electrical device in your circuit panel that cuts power to prevent electrical fires when the AFCI detects minute differences in electrical current caused by punctured wires, shorts, and arcing. See also GFCI.

Ampere (or amp)
An electrical unit of measurement that measures the rate of electrical charge flowing through the system. Electrical service panels and circuit breakers are usually measured in amps.

Arc
A short circuit where the electricity literally jumps, or arcs, to the nearest metal.

B

Backsplash
The wall between the top of a kitchen counter and the bottom of cabinets. Backsplashes, especially behind the kitchen sink, are susceptible to splashing water and must therefore be made of, or covered by, a waterproof or water-resistant material.

Batt
Fibreglass, mineral wool, and cotton insulation are usually sold in rectangular batts of a fluffy material (much like cotton candy). In walls, insulation batts are placed between studs.

Bay
The space between the rafters in an attic.

Building code

The building code sets out the minimum standards for framing and foundations that will ensure that a house is going to be safe and secure. The code is fairly uniform across North America, though there are special provisions in some regions to protect against local dangers such as earthquakes or hurricanes. Separate codes deal with a house's plumbing and electrical systems.

C

Caulk/caulking

Flexible sealant that is used to stop air or water penetration. Caulk comes in many strengths and varieties. The most common caulks are made from latex or silicone.

Centers

Refers to the distance between the middle of two studs (or joists). For example, in modern houses, the distance from the center of one stud to the center of the next stud is usually 16", often spoken of as "16 inches on center," or written as "16" o.c." This distance ensures adequate structural support, and the standard measurement allows for drywall or other coverings to be easily attached to the studs.

Cinder block

Often used in foundations, cinder blocks are made from the ashes of coal or coke bonded by concrete.

Circuit

Electricity flows in a circuit, from the service panel to various outlets and fixtures and then back to the panel. Each circuit is rated for amps, which are controlled by a circuit breaker, commonly 15 or 20 amps. A circuit controlled by a 15-amp breaker is capable of safely carrying 1,440 watts (15 amps x 120 volts x 80% for safety). Ten outlets is usually the maximum for a circuit (fewer if those outlets are serving appliances that draw a lot of electricity, such as window air conditioners).

Circuit breaker

A protective device in an electrical panel that interrupts the flow of electricity in an electrical circuit when there is excess load or a short. Older service panels used fuses, but they were replaced by circuit breakers, which are easier to reset.

Cold zone

An area within a house that isn't heated, such as an attic or crawl space. It's critical that cold zones have proper ventilation to avoid moisture buildup and rot.

Concrete

A construction material made from a mixture of cement, sand, stone, and water. There are many different types of concrete available, and it's critical to use the right one for the job and to not allow concrete to harden too quickly.

Concrete board
A harder, heavier, and more waterproof alternative to drywall, concrete board is made from concrete sandwiched between two layers of fiberglass mesh. Concrete board is advisable for areas with heavy moisture, since it will not mold like regular drywall.

Crawl space
A shallow, unfinished space beneath the first floor of a building. Crawl spaces are sometimes built instead of full-height basements.

Crown
The natural bow in a piece of wood, a visible curve. It's critical when framing a house that all the crowns face the same direction. In a vertical wall, the crowns should face out; on the floor, the crowns should face up.

D

Ditra
A brand-name product from Schluter, Ditra is a waffled orange plastic material that is used under tile to help prevent tiles from cracking.

Drywall
The most common interior wall material, drywall is made from gypsum (a chalk-like mineral) sandwiched between two layers of heavy paper. Drywall comes in many different types and thicknesses, including denser drywalls for ceilings, fire-rated drywalls, and water-resistant and mold-proof drywalls for high-moisture areas. Soundproof drywall is also available.

Drywall compound
Often called "mud," drywall compound is a paste that is used to fill and cover the seams between drywall sheets.

Ducts
The round or rectangular sheet metal pipes in which air flows from a forced air furnace. The main duct from the furnace is called the plenum, and individual ducts run off the plenum to rooms throughout the house.

E

Efflorescence
A white, salty, crystalline deposit commonly seen on foundation walls. The presence of efflorescence is a sign of water invasion in basements.

Engineered wood
Hardwood flooring that is made of three to five layers of wood stacked and bonded together under heat and pressure.

F

Fascia
A long, flat board fastened to the ends of the roofing rafters at the eaves. This is on the exterior of the house.

Feed lines

Plumbing pipes through which water is supplied to the house or to an individual fixture (such as a sink or bathtub). Modern feed lines are usually copper or PEX tubing.

Fiber cement board

Fiber cement board looks like wood, but it's actually a mixture of cement, sand, and cellulose fibers. It can be used in a variety of exterior building materials such as siding or panels.

Fish-eye

Small (but undesirable) air bubbles that may show up in drywall compound as it's applied.

Flashing

The thin sheet metal around the chimney, dormers, skylights, and so forth. In the case of the chimney, for example, the flashing rests flush against the chimney and then goes under the shingles.

Footings

Foundation walls rest on concrete footings, which in turn rest on undisturbed earth. Footings should be twice the width of the wall itself.

Forced air

A common form of heating, featuring a powerful fan that forces warm air throughout the house via ducts in the walls. Forced air furnaces can be powered by natural gas, electricity, propane, or oil.

Foundation

The foundation bears the weight of the house and holds up against the pressure of the earth around it. Foundations can be made of a variety of materials including fieldstone, brick, concrete block, poured concrete, and insulated concrete forms. Foundations are usually dug at least four feet into the ground, below the frost line.

G

GFCI (ground fault circuit interrupter)

This protects people from severe electric shocks and electrocution. A GFCI monitors the amount of current flowing from hot to neutral; if there is a difference—even as small as 4 or 5 milliamps, amounts too small to activate a fuse or circuit breaker—it cuts the electricity in a fraction of a second. See also AFCI.

Grout

A thin mortar for filling joints between tiles. Grout can be cement-based or epoxy.

H

Header

The horizontal beam that carries loads above doors and windows and transfers the weight to the vertical studs on both sides.

House wrap

The sheeting that wraps your home. A house wrap sheds moisture from the outside even while it allows air to flow through its microscopic holes. The air movement allows moisture to move back through to the outside. The most popular house wraps are Tyvek and Typar.

HRV (heat-recovery ventilation unit)

An HRV brings fresh air into the furnace and exhausts stale air. A heat exchanger in the HRV recovers heat from the outgoing air and preheats incoming air to help reduce energy costs.

HVAC

An acronym for the heating, ventilation, and air conditioning systems in a house.

I

ICF (insulated concrete forms)

These foam blocks are reinforced with metal and are filled with concrete as the wall is built, creating a very strong wall with built-in insulation.

Impervious

See Porosity.

J

Jack stud

A second vertical stud used to reinforce the structure of a stud frame wall where a door will be installed.

Joists

Horizontal parallel beams, usually placed on their edge, to support the floors and walls in a house.

Junction box

A metal box where separate lines are run off the circuit to receptacles and lights.

K

Kerdi

A brand-name product from Schluter, Kerdi is a membrane that can be used on floors and walls to create a waterproof barrier before installing stone, ceramic, or porcelain tiles.

Knob and tube

The oldest form of electrical wiring, which was installed until about 1945. The system featured two separate wires—one black and one white—for each circuit, unlike today's electrical wires, which combine black, white, and ground wires. Knob and tube refers to the ceramic knobs the wire was strung from and the tubes used to protect the wire where it passed through joists and studs.

L

Laminate floor

A flooring system comprising interlocking panels. Each panel is made up of an inner core of pressed and glued wood material, with a photographic image of wood laminated on the surface.

Lath

Before drywall became the common choice for interior walls, small slats of wood (lath) were nailed horizontally to the wall studs with a narrow gap between each piece of lath. Thick layers of plaster were then applied to the lath to make a smooth covering.

Lien

A legal claim by one person on another person's property as security on a debt. A contractor (or subcontractor) may place a lien on a house when he has not been paid, so that if the house is sold he is repaid from the proceeds.

Load-bearing wall

A wall that is integral to the construction of the house. It cannot be safely removed without building new supports (various solutions are possible) that will bear an equal or greater load.

M

Mastic

A cement adhesive used to fix tiles to floors, specifically vinyl and linoleum.

MDF (medium density fiberboard)

Because medium density fiberboard doesn't have the structural strength of solid wood or plywood, MDF is not recommended in most renovations, but MDF crown molding and trim are popular lower-cost options.

Mold

A fungus that grows on organic materials such as wood or paper, especially when moisture is present.

Mud

See Drywall compound.

N

Non-vitreous

See Porosity.

O

Off-gassing

Off-gassing happens when chemicals are released into the air by a non-metallic substance such as paint, varnish, or glue. Known as volatile organic compounds (VOCs), the chemicals in off-gases cause a wide range of impacts ranging from relatively mild—stinging eyes, irritated nasal passages, and nausea—to potentially life-threatening.

OSB (oriented strand board)

A modern version of plywood that uses layers of wood flakes, fibers, or strands bonded together under intense heat and pressure. The direction of the fibers alternates between layers for greater strength.

P

Plaster

Common in homes built before the 1940s, plaster is made from gypsum mixed with water and fibrous material. Horsehair was sometimes added to strengthen the plaster before it was applied over wooden lath in plaster-and-lath walls.

PEX

A brand name for a plumbing system that uses flexible plumbing tubes made from aluminum sandwiched between two layers of heat-resistant polyethylene.

Plenum

See Ducts.

Porosity

The ability of a material to absorb water. For stone and tile, porosity is graded using the following system: the least absorbent is called "impervious," followed by "vitreous," "semi-vitreous," and finally the most porous, "non-vitreous."

PVC (polyvinyl chloride)

Plastic used in plumbing pipes (usually white or grey). When it is used as a drainage pipe, PVC connects to the city sewer system or a septic system. When it comes to drain-pipes, the standard rule is ABS for the vent stack and PVC for the in-ground drainage.

R

R-2000

Refers to homes built to a set of energy-efficient standards created by the Canadian government (Natural Resources Canada) and the Canadian Home Builders' Association. Only homes built by specially trained contractors and conforming to the R-2000 standard can be certified as R-2000. Since these homes began to be constructed in the 1970s and 1980s, some problems have arisen, especially with airtightness that leads to moisture and mould growth.

Rigid foam

Not to be confused with white Styrofoam, rigid foam is made from either extruded polystyrene (often seen as pink or blue boards) or expanded polyisocyanurate. Rigid foam is commonly used for insulating foundations and as a thermal and vapor break in basements.

Rough-in

In plumbing and electrical work, rough-in is the stage when an inspection by a building or electrical inspector should occur. The pipes or wires have been installed, but the walls and floors have not been closed in and the fixtures have not been connected.

R-value

The R-value of any material—usually insulation—measures how well that material resists the loss of heat if the temperature on one side of it is higher than on the other side. Basically, the higher the R-value, the better the material insulates.

S

Semi-vitreous

See Porosity.

Service panel

All electricity entering a house first goes into a service panel: a wall-mounted box, usually in the basement, that features breakers for individual circuits.

Soffits

The underside of roof eaves, visible from the ground. Modern soffits are perforated to allow for air movement.

Spalling

The flaking of concrete. A sign of poor-quality material or application.

Stack

See Vent stack.

Stucco

Traditionally a mixture of Portland cement, sand, lime, and water that can be used as a covering for exterior walls. Some newer stucco compounds are not as, if at all, porous.

Stud

One of a series of wood or metal vertical structural members in walls and partitions. Wood studs are usually 2 x 4s, though 2 x 6s are also used, especially for exterior walls, to allow for adequate insulation.

Subfloor

Attached to the supporting joists underneath it, the subfloor is as it sounds: what is below your floor covering. In older houses, the subfloor was often broad planks; in newer houses, it is usually OSB or plywood.

Sump pump

A sump pump commonly refers to both the sump box and sump pump. By code, new houses have a sump box (also known as a well or a pit) underneath the basement floor that collects water from your foundation walls and from under your basement floor. When the box gets full, the sump pump takes the water up and out of the house by means of a pipe that goes through the foundation wall and away from your foundation.

T

Thinset

A mixture of cement, very fine sand, and additives that allow the cement to properly hydrate. Modified thinset has additional polymers added to improve adhesion—basically, it's thinset with more glue.

Truss

A prefabricated triangular roof support. Trusses come in a wide variety of sizes and shapes.

Typar/Tyvek

See House wrap.

U

Underpinning

When lowering a basement floor, under-pinning creates a new, deeper footing (the widest part of the foundation, which the walls sit on) underneath the existing one.

V

Vapor barrier

Usually 6-mil polyethylene plastic sheet, vapor barrier is stapled to the studs on the warm side of an exterior wall (usually this means the interior side of the insulation) to prevent water vapour from getting into the studding.

Vent stack

Also called "the stack" or the "waste and vent stack," the vent stack is a vertical pipe that carries water and waste down to the drainage pipe in the basement. Open at the top and typically sticking out through the roof of your house, the stack also lets sewer gases escape and provides air for drains and toilets to empty properly.

Vitreous

See Porosity.

VOC (volatile organic compounds)

The chemicals in off-gases that cause a wide range of impacts ranging from rela-tively mild—stinging eyes, irritated nasal passages, and nausea—to potentially life-threatening.

Volt

An electrical unit of measurement that measures the electrical pressure exerted by a power source. In Canada, most electrical service is 120 volts or 240 volts.

W

Watts

An electrical unit of measurement that measures the amount of electrical energy flowing to a particular fixture in an electri-cal system. All the lights and devices that you run off your circuits are rated for watt-age—the amount of electricity they con-sume. You see this on light bulbs most ob-viously, but most home appliances—from toasters to TV sets to computers—also give their wattage.

Perforated tile

Not really tile anymore (the original drain-age tile was made of clay), weeping tile is corrugated plastic piping with slits in the top. It is laid around the outside of the foundation to capture excess water and drain it away from the home. The weeping tile connects to the city storm drains. In the suburbs or rural areas, it may be collected into a sump well and then pumped out to ditches.

Photography Credits

INDEX

THE HOLMES FOUNDATION

As our television show continues, we learn more and more about what is actually happening to people renovating their houses. Holmesonhomes.com is flooded with emails every week from people telling us their renovation stories. One of the hardest things we have to do is say "no" to homeowners in trouble. We've learned that there are so many stories out there about jobs gone wrong that we have to pick the biggest projects, the ones where we're trying to salvage the lives of homeowners in trouble. Through these stories we also try to educate people, and maybe teach them how to prevent these renovation disasters in the first place.

But what about the thousands of people we can't help on our show? Who is going to help them? The government is not going to help. Insurance companies are not going to help. Another contractor isn't going to help without charging them—and they don't have the money. They're in trouble. Someone has got to help them. So we're going to do it.

The Holmes Foundation is a charitable organization that has two important goals: We will assist Canadians who need help or resources to get their homes and lives back after botched renovations have seriously endangered their ability to keep their homes; and we promote careers in the trades to young people and their parents, urge employers to hire more apprentices, and offer scholarships and bursaries. We will also develop a roster of professionals—construction lien lawyers, structural engineers, and other experts who will provide assistance to families that have been devastated by a botched renovation.

In Canada there is a desperate—and growing—shortage of skilled workers, and unless youth are encouraged to enter this employment field and employers to train larger numbers of apprentices, homeowners will be increasingly vulnerable to unscrupulous contractors in the future. Without skilled tradespeople who are committed to doing things right, it's too easy for incompetent and unethical contractors to stay in business.

The mission of the Holmes Foundation is to ensure that all residential renovation and construction in Canada is done right . . . the first time. We can make a difference by helping homeowners and by helping the young become the next generation of real pros. I'm going to do everything I can to make sure that happens.

Mike Holmes

To learn more about the Holmes Foundation, please visit www.makeitright.ca.